"Wayne Braudrick's engaging bc really means to be a man: the practices that enable men to be reliable, focused, responsible, chivalrous, wise, loyal, and authentic servant leaders. In this lively and readable book, Braudrick is the superb mentor that makes a convincing case for genuine manhood."

Tom Siems, Ph.D.
Senior Economist, Federal Reserve Bank of Dallas

"Manhood is enlightening and hopeful for men everywhere! Despite living in a culture that minimizes masculinity, Dr. Braudrick shows us example after example of what the biblical definition is of a real man. Gripping, applicable and full of encouragement—Manhood provides steps that every man can take to finally become who God has created him to be!"

John McKinzie
Lead Pastor, Hope Fellowship Churches.

"Wayne Braudrick has done the body of Christ a great service in writing this thoroughly biblical and highly engaging book about manhood. One would be challenged to find a more relevant book for our times. The best thing about it: One cannot read it without being transformed by its message. This book is highly recommended!"

Ron Rhodes, Th.D.
Author and Professor

"I applaud Wayne Braudrick for adding to the literature on masculinity from a biblical perspective. Having raised three young men myself, I am all too keenly acquainted with our secular culture's assault on manhood. We need all the help we can get to stay on track ourselves and help the next generation discover the men God called us all to be."

Bill Peel
Executive Director
Center for Faith & Work at LeTourneau University

ALL THE DIFFERENCE SERIES

Whatever Happened to Manhood?

Forthcoming:

Your Work Matters

In the Name of Love

The Power of a Merry Heart

*To Nineveh—Going Overboard for a
Lost Generation*

WAYNE BRAUDRICK

WHATEVER HAPPENED to MANHOOD?

A Return to Biblical Manhood

LAMPION
Press

Lampion Press, LLC
P. O. Box 932
Silverton, OR 97381

Scripture quotation smarked (NASB) are taken from the New American Standard Bible, Copyright 1960, 1962, 1963, 1968, 1972, 1973, 1975, 1977, 1995 by the Lockman Foundation. Used by permission. (www.Lockman.org)

Scripture quotations marked (NKJV) are taken from the New King James Version®. Copyright © 1982 by Thomas Nelson. Used by permission. All rights reserved.

"Scripture quotations marked (ESV) are from The Holy Bible, English Standard Version® (ESV®), copyright © 2001 by Crossway, a publishing ministry of Good News Publishers. Used by permission. All rights reserved."

Scripture quotations marked (HCSB) are taken from the Holman Christian Standard Bible®, Copyright © 1999, 2000, 2002, 2003, 2009 by Holman Bible Publishers. Used by permission. Holman Christian Standard Bible®, Holman CSB®, and HCSB® are federally registered trademarks of Holman Bible Publishers.

Scripture quotations marked (NLT) are taken from the Holy Bible, New Living Translation, copyright © 1996, 2004, 2007 by Tyndale House Foundation. Used by permission of Tyndale House Publishers, Inc., Carol Stream, IL 60188. All rights reserved.

Scripture quotations marked (TLB) are taken from The Living Bible copyright © 1971. Used by permission of Tyndale House Publishers, Inc., Carol Stream, Illinois 60188. All rights reserved.

Scripture quoted by permission. Quotations designated (NET) are from the NET Bible® copyright ©1996-2006 by Biblical Studies Press, L.L.C. http://netbible.com All rights reserved.

The names: THE NET BIBLE®, NEW ENGLISH TRANSLATION COPYRIGHT (c) 1996 BY BIBLICAL STUDIES PRESS, L.L.C. NET Bible® IS A REGISTERED TRADEMARK THE NET BIBLE® LOGO, SERVICE MARK COPYRIGHT (c) 1997 BY BIBLICAL STUDIES PRESS, L.L.C. ALL RIGHTS RESERVED

ISBN: 978-1-942614-02-9

Library of Congress Control Number: 2015942329

Formatting and cover design by Amy Cole, JPL Design Solutions

Printed in the United States of America

To Benny Braudrick

who first exemplified and taught
these truths to me

CONTENTS

ACKNOWLEDGEMENTS

I am thankful to the Lord who blesses us with all good things to enjoy—even (especially) hard work. And books are hard work! As Solomon pointed out in Ecclesiastes 12, these projects are wearying to the bones. Thanks to Drs. H. Wayne House and Timothy J. Demy of Lampion Press for their encouragement and enthusiasm for this book and series. Thanks to everyone involved with Lampion, including Carrie House and the wonderful Drs. Huffman, and Amy Cole at JPL Design Solutions. Thanks especially to Tim for the brilliant editing.

The team at Frisco Bible Church was invaluable, as always. Roland Gilbert and Jose Portillo designed all the graphics, while Josh Chilton worked his magic on the video end. Regarding publishing, Dr. Ron Rhodes gave excellent wisdom, as always. Randall Satchell, Hayley Dalrymple, Fran Legband, David Wade, Tracy Bush, David Simmonds, and Cynthia Sharp deserve more credit than I can express. Their efforts as a pulpit team—shaping and evaluating these lessons—truly made all the difference. Speaking of "All the Difference," we must acknowledge the ATD board and the Frisco Bible Church Elders, who wisely oversee and fund these efforts for God's glory. Thank you all.

Finally and most significantly, my sweetheart Janna guided this work with amazing grace and wisdom. Our amazing children Jessica, Michael, and Benjamin also helped with wonderful contributions.

FOREWORD

In this book my friend and fellow pastor, Wayne Braudrick, challenges men to live up to biblical standards of manhood. He describes these standards in-depth while offering practical steps to become a man of God. He also uses a number of illustrations—some very personal—but his foundation and frame of reference is the Word of God.

What is behind the diminishment and distortions of manhood? Braudrick believes—and rightly so—that it goes hand in hand with the cultural diminishment and distortions of God Himself! This book reflects a mature analysis. Its tone is serious. It tackles sensitive, important, and challenging topics such as pornography and homosexuality. And it contains the kind of strong bibliography that you would expect to find.

Let's remember that cultural and societal attacks on manhood are not a recent phenomenon. Such attacks began in the Garden of Eden. But thankfully we have the glorious news regarding Christ Jesus who, both human and divine, has modeled in His humanity what it means to be a man's man—and a servant leader!

Gene A. Getz, Ph.D.
Author: *The Measure of a Man*
Professor, Pastor, Author

INTRODUCTION

A BAD SITUATION

The state of affairs for males is increasingly dark. Manliness is frankly unwelcome in most places. The rise of high regard by some for effeminate and homosexual behavior coupled with active disdain from the new feminists has forced masculinity into cultural retreat. Tragically, wanton promiscuity is the only aspect of maleness to escape emasculation. Of course, promiscuity is not even a real sign of manhood but rather an unbiblical, selfish pretense.

Economics also reflect the desperate plight of many males. One fellow in Hanna Rosin's book *The End of Men and the Rise of Women* speaks for many: "All the things we need to be good at to thrive in the world ... are things that my female friends and competitors are better at than me."[1] Though many of the ideas in her book appear laughably overstated and shortsighted, Rosin does expose the feeling of helplessness felt by many men regarding their masculinity.

Further, two inaccurate extremes muddy the waters for Christian thinkers. Patriarchists misapply Scripture through the lens of male superiority and seem to long for some unscriptural utopia where men dominate. At the opposite extreme, feminists misappropriate the term egalitarian and do horrible disservice to both Jewish and Roman history. Both groups practice warped biblical interpretation and wretched history. These opposing and inaccurate forces deepen the current sense of disorientation faced by Christian men and their families.

A RESPONSE

A few years ago, I taught a study at our church titled "Whatever Happened to Manhood?" The results were astonishing. We were flooded with remarkable responses beyond anything I had anticipated. Dedicated feminists voiced sympathetic concerns about the reality and impact of diminishing masculinity in men. Emails from young adult men radiated confidence, saying they now felt motivated and educated about what they are empowered and expected to do. Older men related stories of lessons learned from fathers, grandfathers, and mothers. Single mothers were especially excited, and a number of them downloaded the audio and notes for their fatherless sons to study with them.

Dozens of articles came in—reviews of books, abstracts, and journal pieces—all detailing the issues addressed from Scripture in the *Manhood* series. It seemed as if our entire area was experiencing what my wife calls "new car eyes." One never particularly notices a certain make/model of car on the road, something that changes immediately when you purchase that make/model yourself. After buying one, you suddenly see that car everywhere. So it was with the desperate need for a restoration of biblical manhood in the western world. Everyone seemed to be buying in to God's idea. We all developed "new manhood eyes." For example, a Roman Catholic listener of our radio program shared with me, a Protestant pastor, the following book excerpt, writing: In *The Three Marks of Manhood: How to be Priest, Prophet and King of Your Family*, by G. C. Dilsaver, I came across the following paragraphs that reminded me of the manhood series you recently preached:

> Secular society's hostility toward patriarchy goes hand in hand with its devaluation of motherhood—traditionally considered the essence of feminine character—and its degradation of the family. But the intelligentsia of the twentieth century focused their primary attack on the father figure. Freud said that culture began with "patricide." Mitscherlich asserted that contemporary civilization has progressed into "a fatherless society." And politically we have been told that "emancipation" from patriarchal structures is, according to Marx, a "restoration of humanity and of human relations."

> The resultant ideology of the intelligentsia, in which the term "patriarchy" is strictly a pejorative and where fatherhood is

dead, inevitably finds its way to the mass media and other organs of popular culture. Hence, for example, it is the father who on television is most often targeted for parody or made to play the role of the buffoon. Especially targeted is the father in the form of the Western male ... Very rarely, unless he is to be satirized or villainized in the role, is the Western male given a position of authority, wisdom, or strength. The strategy is clear: cut off the head and the body will wither. By once and for all deposing the traditional Western leader, the Christian father, traditional Western Christian culture will likewise wither away—once and for all.[2]

Dilsaver makes the point that the "disintegration of the West's ancient patriarchal structure," a failing fostered by a "leadership prototype that was a sanitized version of pagan patriarchy rather than a purely Christian one," provides an opportunity for the church to "build a new patriarchy that is based solely on Christ."[3] He further states:

As the traditional Christian family faces its apparent demise, as motherhood is relegated to a secondary status and Christian manhood is at best a parody, as confusion reigns even in regards to sexual identity, Christ demarcates this time as the hour of the family: of motherhood and the home, and of the Christian patriarch ... And now, as the forces of darkness rage against the once-sacrosanct and indomitable institution of the family, chosen men are again called to rise up and wield with manly fortitude and love the singular staff of patriarchy.[4]

The radio listener concluded his note to me writing, "Dr. Braudrick, thank you for helping us understand a 'singular staff' that is biblical and loving instead of harsh and pagan."[5]

That is stirring stuff! By the way, after getting that note, I read the rest of Father Dilsaver's book and found much that was useful. There are some weaknesses and theological differences (especially in his under-standing of Calvinism), but the overall message was inspiring. And the shared inspiration wasn't limited to Christian sources. Another fellow learner sent in this note and excerpt from an article by Charles Murray (the W. H. Brady Scholar at the American Enterprise Institute) in the *Wall Street Journal:*

> Pastor Wayne, this reminded me of the message on men and work:

> It must once again be taken for granted that a male in the prime of life who isn't even looking for work is behaving badly. There can be exceptions for those who are genuinely unable to work or are house husbands. But reasonably healthy working-age males who aren't working or even looking for work, who live off their girlfriends, families or the state, must once again be openly regarded by their fellow citizens as lazy, irresponsible and unmanly. Whatever their social class, they are, for want of a better word, bums.

> To bring about this cultural change, we must change the language that we use whenever the topic of feckless men comes up. Don't call them "demoralized." Call them whatever derogatory word you prefer. Equally important: Start treating the men who aren't feckless with respect. Recognize that the guy who works on your lawn every week is morally superior in this regard to your neighbor's college-educated son who won't take a "demeaning" job. Be willing to say so.

> This shouldn't be such a hard thing to do. Most of us already believe that one of life's central moral obligations is to be a productive adult. The cultural shift that I advocate doesn't demand that we change our minds about anything; we just need to drop our nonjudgmentalism.

> It is condescending to treat people who have less education or money as less morally accountable than we are. We should stop making excuses for them that we wouldn't make for ourselves. Respect those who deserve respect, and look down on those who deserve looking down on.[6]

And so the rich dialogues continued. Eventually, a friend mentioned how useful this study could be for a broader audience than our little world in North Texas. That led to a series of prayers, conversations, revamped Bible studies, recordings, further discussions, and finally, the book you are holding. Regardless of whether you are male or female, I pray that this will grant you new manhood eyes as well.

CHAPTER 1

A REAL MAN KEEPS HIS WORD

CHAPTER SUMMARY: Males and females both need to be reminded to keep their word, but men in particular are assaulted by an eternal adolescence in our society that applauds unreliability. In contrast to that worldly message, God's Word calls men to make a difference in the world by being trustworthy. The wise person discovers Jesus the promise keeper to be the ultimate example of and empowerment for personal faithfulness.

LIFE CHANGE OBJECTIVE: That we are reliable.

"DUDE, NOBODY IS RELIABLE ANYMORE."

I have a pastor friend who calls me every few years just to ask: "Wayne, are you still a man of integrity? Have you slept only with Janna? Have you not stolen any money or abused power?" When I answer him that—by God's grace—I am still clean, he always says, "Thank God. I think we're the only ones. Dude, nobody is reliable anymore."

Now, he's wrong in the same way Elijah was wrong as recorded in 1 Kings 19. Elijah had just emerged from a stirring and yet harrowing experience on Mt. Carmel. Standing alone against the massed priests of the detestable god Baal (whose worship greatly appealed to the sexual appetites of the culture), Elijah had partnered with God in a mighty display of power. Yet immediately after that triumph, Elijah was suddenly on the run for his life. Cultural elites do not appreciate having the emptiness of their belief system exposed, and the full wrath of Israel's king and queen was immediately directed toward Elijah. The prophet ran for his life, ending up far away and alone in a cave.

Look at Elijah's subsequent conversation with God:

> *Elijah:* 1 Kings 19:14 "I am the only one left, and now they are trying to kill me, too." (NLT)

> *God:* "Yet I will preserve 7,000 others in Israel who have never bowed down to Baal or kissed him!" (NLT)

We're not alone standing for the Lord's truth. Wonderfully, there are millions of trustworthy people in the world. But my friend is right in this—the reliable ones are a small percentage of the world population. And that percentage gets smaller every year. In our place and time, trustworthiness is in deep decline and it is a decline that seems to steepen with each new generation.

Look at these recent numbers from a study by the Josephson Institute of Ethics[7]:

- 51% of teenagers 17 and under believe that lying and cheating are necessary to succeed. Compare that with people over 50 years of age: only 10% of them believe lying and cheating are necessary.

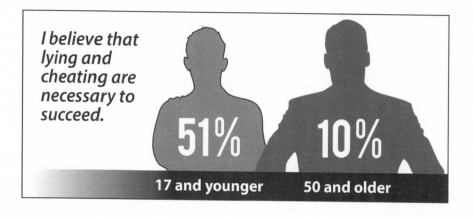

I believe that lying and cheating are necessary to succeed.

51%   10%

17 and younger   50 and older

- This current generation of young men is nearly four times as likely to deceive their boss—31% of teens say they lie to a boss as opposed to 8% of those over 50.

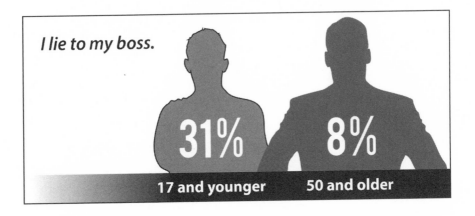

- 49% of the under-17 group say they keep change mistakenly given to them—49%! Compare that with only 15% of their parents and grandparents.

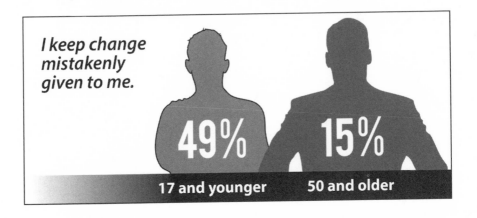

- While it's appalling that 18% of the older men in America believe it's acceptable to lie to one's spouse about something significant, look at the numbers for the coming generation—48% of them say it's appropriate to lie to one's spouse about something important.

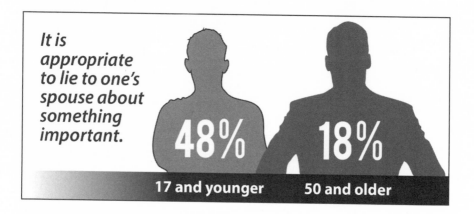

It is appropriate to lie to one's spouse about something important.

48%   **18%**

17 and younger   **50 and older**

Now just in case you think that these answers are merely "boys being boys;" if you think these are youthful responses that will change over time; I have some sobering news. The Josephson Institute of Ethics has found that under-17 attitudes on integrity are excellent predictors for later actions in middle age.

They followed a bunch of survey respondents for 20 years after their original answers, and uncovered some amazing truths about people. They found that unreliable boys remain boys late in life. Here's the data[8]:

- Compared to those who never cheated, high school cheaters are three times more likely to lie to a customer—20% *vs.* 6% of people who didn't cheat as teenagers.

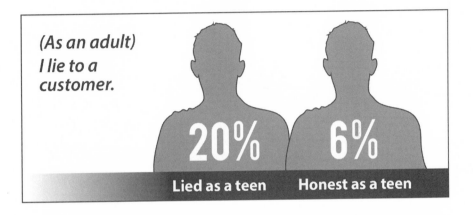

(As an adult) I lie to a customer.

20% 6%

Lied as a teen   Honest as a teen

- People who rejected integrity as youths are more than twice as likely to inflate an expense claim—10% *vs.* 4% of those who didn't steal in high school. Understand also that this is *self-reported*. The real numbers are no doubt much higher.

(As an adult) I have inflated expense claims.

10% 4%

Stole as a teen   Did not steal as a teen

- People who eschew integrity when they are young are twice as likely to lie to or deceive their boss. 20% of them say they lie to their bosses as grown-ups ... *vs.* 10% of others.

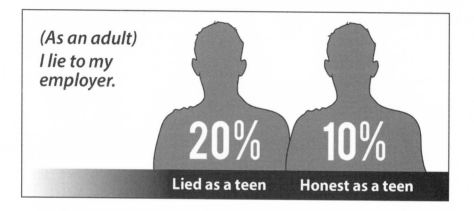

(As an adult) I lie to my employer.

20% — Lied as a teen   10% — Honest as a teen

- After they are adults, 35% of young men who regularly lied in high school admit that they lie to their spouse or significant other. That's compared with 22% of the population at large.

(As an adult) I lie to my spouse or significant other.

35% — Lied as a teen   22% — Honest as a teen

The pattern is clear. Attitudes about integrity when one is young are excellent predictors of trustworthiness in later life. And remember, the coming generation of men is comprised of a majority that believes cheating and lying are necessary for success. Integrity is on a steep decline that has very serious consequences for the future.

MEN WHO MAKE A DIFFERENCE ARE TRUSTWORTHY (EXODUS 18:21-23).

Now you are no doubt wondering, "So, what in the world can we do about it? What should we do about this looming 'integrity cliff?'" I'm so glad you asked! Open your Bible to the second book—Exodus—and let's look at part of God's answer. Context is always important in order to properly understand Scripture, and the back-story here contains a monumental scene. Moses is leading the people of Israel on their way to the Promised Land. They're crawling along with millions of people, their animals, their physical and emotional baggage, and their struggles and problems. And everybody is bringing those problems to Moses. Finally, they stop close to the lands of Moses' brilliant father-in-law, Jethro. Jethro comes over, sees how things are going, and gives some of the best leadership advice in history. Let's pick up Jethro's advice in verses 21-23:

> Furthermore, you shall select out of all the people able men who fear God, men of truth, those who hate dishonest gain; and you shall place these over them, as leaders of thousands, of hundreds, of fifties and of tens. And let them judge the people at all times; and let it be that every major dispute they will bring to you, but every minor dispute they themselves will judge. So it will be easier for you, and they will bear the burden with you. If you do this thing and God so commands you, then you will be able to endure, and all these people also will go to their place in peace." (NASB)

Moses has an opportunity to get the people an enduring peace. And the key aspect to lasting peace involves finding men who are trustworthy. Jethro teaches Moses that the men who make a difference are trustworthy. Look at the three statements of character in verse 21: able men who fear God, men of truth, those who hate dishonest gain.

These are not liars. They speak truth. They are not willing to keep change given to them by accident. They do not bribe or steal. They are haters of dishonest gain. They fear God.

One of my favorite little business books of the twentieth century was *Small Decencies* by John Cowan, an ex-Roman Catholic priest-turned HR consultant. Listen to what he says on this subject:

> I know that over the years I have gained a reputation for integrity. My friends expect me to take the risk of saying what I see, doing what I must, being who I am. I have my flaws, but this is seen as my strength. Let me now tell you my secret … I fear God. I fear God and my family. When the question is asked, the situation developed, the powerful awaiting my answer, I see a ghostly party pause, my family waiting expectantly in silence. And whenever I have said what I must say or done what I must do, whatever the response in the [visible] room, I hear an invisible chorus … I hear God say "well done, good and faithful servant!" I hear my family chorus descant: "What a big boy he is!" "Just like his mother!" "His father might have said that!" It is not that I am uninfluenced by the opinions of others, but I fear and respect God and my family chorus more than anyone I have ever met. And that's how I stay who I am.[9]

Cowan is exactly correct. Lasting business impact is dependent on finding trustworthy people with whom to deal. And how does one find such people? You look for what God told Moses to seek: able men who fear God, men of truth, those who hate dishonest gain.

TRUSTWORTHINESS IS TIED TO AN ATTITUDE OF RESPECT TOWARD GOD (LUKE 16:10-13).

Jesus addresses the same concept in His famous parable in Luke 16. For our purposes here, we'll skip the parable and get to Jesus' commentary in verses 10-13:

> "He who is faithful in a very little thing is faithful also in much; and he who is unrighteous in a very little thing is

unrighteous also in much. If therefore you have not been faithful in the use of unrighteous mammon, who will entrust the true riches to you? And if you have not been faithful in the use of that which is another's, who will give you that which is your own? No servant can serve two masters; for either he will hate the one, and love the other, or else he will hold to one, and despise the other. You cannot serve God and mammon." (NASB)

The person who is faithful in little things—like keeping his word—tells you by such small issues that he can be trusted with bigger things. And in God's economy, that then leads to eternal blessing; to entrusting with the things that *really* matter.

Note this concept central to both Jethro's and Jesus' teaching: all this trustworthiness is tied to an attitude of respect toward God. When a person serves God as the primary focus of his days, that person will be faithful, trustworthy, and reliable. If he isn't trustworthy in the little things of life, then it's a reasonable conclusion that the man doesn't really live in fear of God. When you don't obey God's Word in the little things He's shared with us, it's obvious that you don't respect the Lord enough to be trusted with bigger things.

Years ago, I was about to hire my first pastoral staff member. I was completely intimidated by the idea and met with Dr. J. Dwight Pentecost of Dallas Theological Seminary (yes, that was his real name) to get his thoughts on what to look for in a pastor. "Dr. P." was very succinct: "Here's the biggest thing: don't hire any pastor who can't live within his means. If he can't handle his own salary—however large or small—without racking up debt, then he can't handle the riches of God's church."

The people who make a difference are trustworthy with little things like money ... and also with *words*. That's why a wise men's ministry builds so much of the work around 2 Timothy 2:2:

You have heard me teach many things that have been confirmed by many reliable witnesses. Teach these great truths to trustworthy people who are able to pass them on to others. (NLT)

Jesus, Paul, and Moses are all saying the same thing. The world gets changed through the work of trustworthy people.

HEALING COMES THROUGH AMBASSADORS WHO KEEP THEIR WORD (PROVERBS 13:17).

The book of Proverbs has an interesting take on this subject. For example, consider the representative sample of Proverbs 13:17 from the King James Version:

> A wicked messenger falleth into mischief: but a faithful ambassador is health. Healing comes through ambassadors who keep their word.

When I was sixteen years old, I got my first job that didn't involve physical labor. A sporting goods retailer that had four shops in the area where I lived hired me. I shook hands ... encouraged wrestlers to come in to the store ... strung tennis rackets ... sold shoes ... and generally enjoyed working in air conditioning.

I had been at the store less than three months, when the GM came to our store and said, "Wayne, you're now going to be the messenger that runs between the four stores. You'll drive a van and take products needed by customers at other stores ... Also, you're going to take the deposits from each store each day and ferry them to our bank downtown."

I said, "Yes sir." But then I added, "Um ... sir ... you know I'm only 16 years old, right? Are you sure you want me driving tens of thousands of dollars around?" The fellow looked at me and said, "Listen son. You have no idea how rare a trustworthy employee is. No idea. Someday, when you are hiring people you'll understand. Wayne," he continued, "when you have someone that you can trust to be honest you send them to every store every day. Their attitude is like an infection—a good infection. You want as many people as possible to come in contact with them."

I immediately asked for a raise and was told to get back to work. Now, look at what the boss said and compare his experiential wisdom with God's truth in Proverbs 13:17. Amazingly similar, aren't they!

THE BEST SERVANT-LEADERS CAN WITHSTAND THE MOST SEVERE AUDIT (DANIEL 6:3-4).

The prophet Daniel also exemplifies the big idea that people who make a difference are trustworthy. Look at Daniel 6:3-4:

> Then this Daniel began distinguishing himself among the commissioners and satraps because he possessed an extraordinary spirit, and the king planned to appoint him over the entire kingdom. Then the commissioners and satraps began trying to find a ground of accusation against Daniel in regard to government affairs; but they could find no ground of accusation or evidence of corruption, inasmuch as he was faithful, and no negligence or corruption was to be found in him. (NASB)

This is Daniel's last great posting in his life, and it proves an important point: The best servant-leaders can withstand the most severe audit. Can you imagine surviving a full-on scrutiny like that? Probably only people running for president of the United States face that level of scrutiny today. Save the jokes about presidents and just note the point—Daniel was found clean even when they scoured every part of his life. These bad guys were sitting around plotting how they could possibly disembowel Daniel, no doubt physically as well as politically.

And so they dissected the man of God's life, only to find him completely clean. Yet, Daniel is not a hero in this world. Male heroes in the world are guys who get away with extended adolescent irresponsibility. The world seems to like it that way. Men who play the lying, foolish sit-com man-child are applauded. But guys who stand up as godly, reliable men—they are often made fun of by others. They are feared like the Persians feared Daniel. Maybe that's why people of reliability, faithfulness, and trustworthiness are such an endangered species.

The world is changed through men who say what they mean and mean what they say. But that's an extraordinary trait, an increasingly rare quality in these days. That paucity explains one reason why we're going through this study together.

Consider the premise for our study:

Premise [why we are studying this]: Women and men today are desperately confused about masculinity. Our global antagonism toward all things male furiously sucks all joy out of normative human interaction and leaves both sexes in a quandary regarding fulfilling relationships. Our widespread abandonment of biblical manhood has not just decimated masculinity, but has harmed femininity as well. Women are left aching for what God declares important—real men—and find their own peace and happiness declining. Wonderfully, God cares about men and women and bestows clear biblical solutions that cut through the nonsense and allow men to be all He intends.

Now, before someone writes to accuse me of being a misogynist, please know that it is mostly *women* who are writing today about the decline of manhood and the subsequent slide in female happiness. Here's just one recent example by Mary Eberstadt:

Why do the pages of our tonier magazines brim with mournful titles like "The Case for Settling" and "The End of Men?" Why do websites run by and for women focus so much on men who won't grow up, and ooze such despair about relations between the sexes?

Why do so many accomplished women simply give up these days and decide to have children on their own, sometimes using anonymous sperm donors, thus creating the world's first purposely fatherless children? What of the fact, widely reported earlier this week, that 26% of American women are on some kind of mental-health medication for anxiety and depression and related problems?

Or how about what is known in sociology as "the paradox of declining female happiness?" Using 35 years of data from the General Social Survey, two Wharton School economists, Betsey Stevenson and Justin Wolfers, made the case in 2009 that women's happiness appeared to be declining over time despite their advances in the work force and education.[10]

Why are we studying biblical manhood? Our goal is nothing less than the joy and health of *women*. Today, women and men need change. And that change begins with men who keep their word.

The talented team that helps me develop these materials also crafted an objective for this study:

Objective [what we hope to see God accomplish in us through the study]: That we actively encourage godly manliness.

Pastor Crawford Loritts at Fellowship Bible Church in Roswell, Georgia comments on this. He writes, "As a pastor, I witness daily the void and dysfunction caused by men who don't really know who and what a man is."[11]

When I first started teaching as a career, I never foresaw that a book like this would be necessary. But today this has become a must! Many of you guys who are reading this did not grow up with a father who lived out what the Bible says about manhood. Even though you can't change the past, you can and must break that cycle. You have the chance to prosper as a man according to God's direction—something that will make all the difference for you and all who love you and know you.

Many of you incredibly strong moms are raising sons on your own. You need to know how the process is supposed to turn out. Every one of us has interaction with men and women around us—people who need to see and hear what real masculinity is all about. So we're going to work together toward this goal. And here's how it's going to flow—look at our series theme:

Theme of the study [what the series is about]: Men can reclaim manhood!

They needn't fall into misogyny or feminization; rather men can live out their masculinity just the way God directs. This is desperately important for each male, his family and friends, and the larger culture around us. Though the days appear very difficult, the world actually longs for guys who make an impact as real men of God. This study will teach men (and those who love them) how to live out our birthright as males.

RALIABILL

For as long as there have been people, humans have tried to describe themselves. The things that drove our ancestors to depict their character are the same forces that motivate our speech today. For example, in medieval Scotland, they combined two words from other languages to make a new unified concept. *Rely*—a word that meant to lean on—was added to *Able*—an English suffix for capacity or ability.

Rely was originally a French military word from the Middle Ages. It came from Latin words for feudal attachments that could be trusted. A lord could rely on his knights, and the knights could fall back on their lord. They could rely on each other. They could *rally* together.

Able is a strange word in English. Old Latin had a way to depict capacity for something. You would take a verb and add *–ible* to the end. That would show ability. For example, if something has the ability to be accessed, that thing is "accessible."

Yet, medieval English writers thought the *–ible* ending looked funny. So they modified the Latin practice and made an *–able* ending instead. *–Able* was their way of representing capacity. For example, if something had the ability to be altered, it became "alterable."

With that in mind, let's go back to Scotland during the years of their wars with their neighbors. The Scots wanted to find a way to describe men that could be counted on ... men who would rally to the clan ... men who protected the persecuted Christians of Scotland ... men who would not become traitors. They needed a word to describe *Bravehearts* who wouldn't sell out to the English ... men who wouldn't expose where the Scottish Christians met in secret.

So, they came up with this new gem of a word: *raliabill.* It was the capacity to be trusted—in battle, in church, and in life. Of course, such need continued through the ages. Contemporary people needed a way to describe humans who can be trusted responsibly to come through for each other. Our more recent forebears needed a word for men who keep their word regardless of how difficult or painful it might be to do so.

In the 1850s Americans took that Scottish word, cleaned up the spelling, and started using *"reliable."* They decided that reliability is just as critical in each of our lives as it was for our Christian forefathers in Scotland. You and I need to rely on people just as much as those medieval Frenchmen and those classical Romans. Reliability is a critical need for our time—as it has been for every age.

That's why the word was later drafted for use in engineering, computer science, and psychology—reliability is a critical human need. However, in our day human reliability is in such steep decline that it appears to be in free fall. As we saw in the earlier statistics and no doubt personally experience frequently, a reliable man is hard to find.

GOD'S STRENGTH ENABLES A MAN'S FAITHFULNESS (I CORINTHIANS 7:25B).

But, please do not despair, friends! God has given us the key to reversing this decline. It's found in 1 Corinthians 7:25. In this little statement tucked away in a longer discussion, the Apostle Paul gives us a key to healthy manliness:

> I give an opinion as one who by the mercy of the Lord is trustworthy. (NASB)

God's strength enables a man's faithfulness. With that in mind, look in Exodus 18. There's a really significant Hebrew word used in verse 21, where we read:

> "Furthermore, you shall select out of all the people able men
> who fear God, men of truth, those who hate dishonest gain;
> and you shall place these over them, as leaders of thousands,
> of hundreds, of fifties and of tens." (NASB)

Chayil (khah' il) is the term we translate *"able."* It's a very important and powerful word in Hebrew. It means *"force."* It was a term used for someone who had force or impact. The same term is used of one of the greatest men in history—Boaz, the husband of Ruth and grandsire of King David. Ruth 2:1 tells us:

Ruth 2:1 Now Naomi had a relative of her husband's, a worthy man of the clan of Elimelech, whose name was Boaz. (ESV)

"Worthy man" in Hebrew is *"gibowr chayil,"* which is literally, *"a powerful force."* *Chayil* was often used of wealth, but it's more than money. It was used of political power. The text is telling us that Boaz is a powerful man of force.

Now, with that biblical history in mind, go back to Rabbi Saul's (the Apostle Paul) New Testament statement in 1 Corinthians 7:25b.

I give an opinion as one who by the mercy of the Lord is trustworthy. (NASB)

Wise men—real men who change the world—know that their force doesn't come from themselves. It is not their flesh that makes them people of impact. Real influence comes from the Lord's merciful power in the inner person. Our trustworthiness doesn't come from ourselves. It is empowered from God the Holy Spirit.

I love how Jackie Kendall summarizes this in her book *A Man Worth Waiting For.* Jackie describes two basic kinds of men in the world—Bozo and Boaz. This clever demarcation comes from the Bible and American pop culture. Bozo was a television clown in the 1950s-60s while Boaz is one of the great heroes of the Bible—second husband to Ruth and grandsire of King David. Kendall says that Bozos are everywhere. They may talk a nice game, but they never keep their word. Bozos are unreliable because their power comes only from themselves.

Too often, females set themselves up to fall for Bozo after Bozo. Here's my favorite comment Jackie makes. It comes in a chapter titled "Don't be bozo bait" in which she writes:

Being driven more by culture than by the ultimate Love Manual [the Bible] makes you terribly vulnerable to bad relationships. To find God's best and resist Bozo, you need to be grounded in biblical truths, not Hollywood fantasies. This biblical core will form an internal radar system that alerts you quickly to Bozos and will sustain you as you hold out for a Boaz … the Bible's "instructions are not mere words—they are your life!" (Deuteronomy 32:47 NLT)[12]

Women, do not settle for a Bozo! Boaz is a redemptive fellow, as one can see in the biblical book named for his wife Ruth. Boaz was thoughtful, other-centered, wise, industrious, and powerful. In fact, power is the main factor in the life of a Boaz. He is a man of power—power that comes from God the Holy Spirit.

Guys, you may have been horribly unreliable in the past. You may not have been a man of your word. Maybe you have even broken your vows to God and people. In all honesty you may look in the mirror and be forced to confess that you are more of a Bozo than a Boaz. So, listen carefully. The restoration of God awaits you. You can right now begin your transformation from Zero to Hero.

And it doesn't have anything to do with more strength *from* you. It has everything to do with you relying on God's strength *for* you. We desperately need Boaz-like men! Do you want to be one? If so, then you must learn to fully rely on God. Learn and live out the truth that His power enables your faithfulness.

About the time that the new word "reliable" was becoming fashionable, Josiah Gilbert Holland—first editor of *Scribner's Monthly* (later the *Century Magazine*)—wrote a poem in which he tried to capture the import of 1 Corinthians 7:25 in the lives of males. Look at his poem "Wanted":

GOD give us men! A time like this demands
Strong minds, great hearts, true faith and ready hands;
Men whom the lust of office does not kill;
　Men whom the spoils of office can not buy;
Men who possess opinions and a will;
　Men who have honor,—men who will not lie;
Men who can stand before a demagogue
　And damn his treacherous flatteries without winking!
Tall men, sun-crowned, who live above the fog
　In public duty, and in private thinking;
For while the rabble, with their thumb-worn creeds,
Their large professions and their little deeds,—

Mingle in selfish strife, lo! Freedom weeps,
Wrong rules the land and waiting justice sleeps!

Do you see that? Real men trample self beneath them. They know that being full of God's Spirit is the key to manhood. These men—men the world needs—keep their word! They will not lie.

FAITHFULNESS IS IMPORTANT IN EVERYONE (I TIMOTHY 3:11).

Of course this isn't something we need only from men. I am only emphasizing reliability for guys because we have a culture that exalts *un*faithfulness in men. We all know that faithfulness is actually important in everyone, male and female. 1 Timothy 3 makes this clear:

> Women must likewise be dignified, not malicious gossips,
> but temperate, faithful in all things. (NASB)

Whether these women are deaconesses or the wives of church leaders is a fascinating discussion that matters not at all for our purposes here. Whatever their role, Paul points out how important it for *everyone* to be faithful in all things.

After my original message on this topic went to iTunes, I received some mail from a broad range of people who study along with our church. The letters claimed that faithfulness really isn't that important. Some of them remarked that keeping one's word is a quaint old concept that doesn't actually affect the bottom line in business or leadership.

In reply, I asked them to examine just one news day from 2012. On November 9, 2012 the following message was released to the CIA workforce:

> Yesterday afternoon, I went to the White House and asked the President to be allowed, for personal reasons, to resign from my position as D/CIA. After being married for over 37 years, I showed extremely poor judgment by engaging in an extramarital affair. Such behavior is unacceptable, both as a husband and as the leader of an organization such as

ours. This afternoon, the President graciously accepted my resignation.

With admiration and appreciation,
David H. Petraeus[13]

On the exact same day, Doug Cameron of the *Wall Street Journal* broke this story:

> Just hours after Washington was rocked by the surprise resignation of General David Petraeus … Lockheed Martin Corp. ousted its incoming chief executive, Christopher Kubasik, for having a "close personal relationship" with a subordinate at the defense contractor. The company said Mr. Kubasik, who is married, was asked to resign Friday after an investigation determined the "improper conduct" violated Lockheed's code of ethics.[14]

Might you still think faithfulness isn't important? Go ask those families. Ask all the people who work for Lockheed Martin or the CIA. Or listen to this brilliant history lesson from Roman Catholic business consultant, John Cowan:

> We have short memories. The business culture of the United States was founded by Puritans and their fellow travelers. They did discuss God at the office, and they did discuss business in church. One reason that they were so willing to develop and embrace a marketplace without government control, a marketplace where each individual could operate freely without confining legal boundaries, was that they themselves were thoroughly controlled by the common morality and tenets of a deeply held and persistently reinforced religion.
>
> When they visualized economic and business freedom, they visualized the freedom of men already held under restraint. They would have been horrified at leveraged buyouts. "What has this man added to creation?" they would have asked. "What good has he done?" they could not imagine a

man so free from religious restraint that he would seek benefit without contribution. When such men were found, they were held without honor, rejected from the community of the church and the community of other businessmen. Such people were certainly not to be regarded as worthy of praise simply because their dealings created personal wealth.

Businessmen of that day were not businessmen from expediency, they were businessmen by vocation. As the preacher had been called to preach, the teacher called to teach, they were called by God to run a business. They approached their task with the intensity of purpose and the rigid ethics of a celibate monk. Quite successfully, too.[15]

When you meet anybody who doesn't believe integrity is needed—for our men, women, children, and world—just read them that essay.

CHANGE IS NOT IMPOSSIBLE AND IT BEGINS WITH US.

There was a second kind of letter that I received about this presentation. It came from defeated Christians crying out variations on the theme: "The hill is too steep! There's no way we can really make any lasting difference in a culture that is this disparaging of masculine integrity."

While agreeing with the seriousness of the battle, I respectfully submitted that hopelessness is misguided. In the immortal words of Miracle Max in the *Princess Bride*, the patient is only "mostly dead." By God's grace, we can make the real cultural change that desperately needs to be made. Yes, it will be slow; but it can also be exponential. If only 1000 people studying this will defend, protect, and exemplify God's idea of manhood, it can start a massive change.

Imagine that 1000 of us are confronted with two opportunities over the next months. Twice in conversations we say something like, "Yes, that joke is funny. But you know men don't have to be unreliable like that. I know a lot of guys who are really godly and wise and trustworthy."

Now suppose only half of the people we're talking to agree to rethink our current cultural poor idea of manhood. Do you know what that means? It means that in months we have 2000 people who are willing to support biblical manhood.

Then, over the next three months each of those 2000 engages in two conversations. Let's assume porn is involved and our 2000 witnesses say the truth:

> Dude. That is not manly. That's nowhere close. I heard this speech recently that you need to hear. They guy showed how counterfeit that is and how important *real* manliness is. I'll send you the link.

OK, suppose half of those folks get it. Now we have 4000 defenders in just six months. It's slow but exponential. Continue our example and after nine months we have 8000 people showing the power and goodness of scriptural manliness. And during the next three months, those 8000 each talk to two people. When men are automatically accused of all being rapists[16], they each say, "Girl. You got it all wrong. Real manhood is not a detriment to female actualization. They aren't in our way! We need them." Let's say only half of their audiences accept God's truth. That's a low percentage, I know. But at the end of one year we have changed 16,000 hearts. Now carry that forward for three years and have just two significant conversations each quarter. At the end of three years, we have impacted 4 million people.

Do you know what that means? It means that a baby boy born today has a real chance of going to a kindergarten where he won't automatically feel marginalized like the man in Hannah Rosin's quote at the beginning of this book's Introduction. It means a girl graduating high school today has a good chance of meeting a godly man who knows what it means to grow with her in faithful marriage as God intended it. It means that God used *us* to create a healthier world! That can and should begin right now in each of us. And it all starts with being people of integrity.

CHAPTER 2

A REAL MAN
KEEPS HIS FOCUS

> CHAPTER SUMMARY: The Apostle Paul teaches us all how to run the life race victoriously. People of God must keep their focus! Specifically, we must remain focused on truth; stay in control, keep looking to the end results, concern ourselves with pleasing God, sacrifice self, stay immersed in Scripture, and avoid grumpiness.
>
> LIFE CHANGE OBJECTIVE: That we stay focused to the end.

THE OLD COACH TAUGHT ME A VALUABLE LESSON.

I walked off the mat at a big Junior High wrestling tournament, and there was this really old guy (to me) waiting to speak with me. He was about fifty years old, and everybody around sort of genuflected and called him "Coach." He introduced himself as Stan Abel, head wrestling coach at the University of Oklahoma. I shook his hand and he walked me over to a practice mat. And while we sat together on that mat, that coach taught me a valuable lesson about wrestling—a lesson that has applied to life far beyond the mat.

Coach Abel looked at me and said, "Wayne, you have the speed and the brains, but you need to perfect focus. Focus is the great key to success."

Then Coach Abel walked me through a series of exercises designed to increase my focus and increase my effectiveness. I learned to control every situation by first controlling myself. As I sharpened my focus with all those exercises, I began to succeed like never before. I began to dream about matches. I would study my opponent very carefully and then wrestle him dozens of times in my sleep according to his tendencies. I learned to tune out all the voices in a gym, except the ones I needed to hear. It got to where I could hear nothing except my coach and my father. The other hundreds of voices were mute to my ears.

Unforunately, an injured neck kept me from ever wrestling for Coach Abel or any other college coach. But he successfully passed the focus baton to me. He taught me what I mastered. I then taught the same disciplines to a bunch of students that I coached. They are basically the same truths I am teaching to you today, summarized in the word "focus." Focus is critical if you are going to succeed in life. You must learn to focus.

This is a study on biblical manhood, but that doesn't affect the applicability of this lesson for women. Females need to work on focus as well. Ladies, this lesson is equally for you. "So then," you may be wondering, "why place this discussion inside a manhood series?" That's a great question!

We're addressing focus as part of the manliness study because you and I inhabit a time and place where males are *expected* to lose focus and are *applauded* for being distracted. Our current culture produces male losers greatly because it reinforces lack of focus in men. Wonderfully, the common culture generally admires the focused woman. Yet the focused male is considered a threat, causing men to subtly and steadily lose their capacity for single-mindedness. That must change.

THE APOSTLE PAUL IS A POSTER-CHILD FOR FOCUS.

You needn't take my word for what I've just written. If you read 2 Timothy 4 you will see the lesson brilliantly expounded by God through His Apostle Paul. 2 Timothy 4 contains important wisdom from an old wrestler. An aged Paul is handing the baton off to Timothy and he wants to make certain that Tim knows how to focus. He starts off discussing Timothy's calling to pastor:

> I solemnly charge you in the presence of God and of Christ
> Jesus, who is to judge the living and the dead, and by His
> appearing and His kingdom: preach the word; be ready in
> season and out of season; reprove, rebuke, exhort, with great
> patience and instruction. (NASB)

Now, that's a substantive calling, though of course not all of us are set
aside to be pastors. However, we are all called to run this race as followers of Jesus. And the next two verses deal with the importance of keeping one's focus in a world where dedication and concentration don't
come easily. Paul describes the wrestling match of life focus. He details
how all around are trying their best to get you off-task, to wrestle you
to the ground. He writes:

> For the time will come when they will not endure sound
> doctrine; but wanting to have their ears tickled, they will
> accumulate for themselves teachers in accordance to their
> own desires; and will turn away their ears from the truth,
> and will turn aside to myths. (NASB)

Let's consider these verses further.

STAY FOCUSED ON TRUTH (VSS. 3-4).

People don't want to listen to truth. I know that I often don't!
Denial is not just a river in Africa. It's a part of the human condition.
What's most odd is that people will work very hard to get teachers who
make them feel happy about their preconceived notions—notions that
cannot stand up to biblical reason. We've all known ear-ticklers. No
doubt you can think of many examples. When we contemplate such
shallow people, there's one thing we probably think of foremost. We say
to ourselves, "Thank goodness I'm not like that!"

But we can be like that, can't we? You and I are perfectly capable
of losing focus because we fall for the popular deceptions of our days.
Right? It's not just *others* who fall for nonsense that sounds attractive.
So, let's not pretend we are somehow immune to that take-down. Let's
instead prepare ourselves to stay focused on truth by thinking through
some popular lies that assail us today. Let's cover three of them quickly:

#1—If you want to keep yourself focused on truth, then, steer clear of mysterious "secrets."

Let me make an easy prediction: at some point during the next five years, there will be some best-selling book that claims to reveal a great, previously-hidden truth about God. How do I know? Because that kind of nonsense takes over the best-seller lists at least once every five years. Someone will have a dream ... a near-death experience ... receive some supposedly secret angelic revelation ... find special computer-generated hidden message in the Bible ... or some other sensational experience.

And it's all hogwash! Paul says keep your eyes fixed on biblical truth, not myths. He addressed this in his earlier letter to Timothy as well. Look at 1 Timothy 4:6-7:

> In pointing out these things to the brethren, you will be a
> good servant of Christ Jesus, constantly nourished on the
> words of the faith and of the sound doctrine which you have
> been following. But have nothing to do with worldly fables
> fit only for old women. On the other hand, discipline your-
> self for the purpose of godliness. (NASB)

Fill your head with clear Bible truth and not speculative old wives' tales. We should also deal with another popular lie of our time: sexual confusion.

#2—If you want to remain focused on truth keep your head clear of sexual confusion.

We live in a time when it's considered the height of correctness to blur the lines between men and women. Sadly, those who fill their head with such foolishness inevitably become antagonistic toward God's people. They will eventually grow hostile toward God's Word as well. That's why Paul writes the following words to men in 1 Corinthians 16:13-14:

> Be watchful, stand firm in the faith, act like men, be strong.
> Let all that you do be done in love. (ESV)

Friends, it's really simple. When you trust God whose Scripture unequivocally declares that humans are male and female, then you are in a position to live all of life in a spirit of love. When you trust God and act appropriately for your sex (male or female), then you can love males and females. You can stand strong in love.

But if you start confusing sexual identities ... if you pretend that women or men should act like each other ... if you denigrate females or disparage masculinity (each of which is very popular in our day) ... then you will become unloving—period. Verse 14 flows out of verse 13.

This is why the ugliest hate mail I get is not from atheists. It's not from Muslims. I get interesting letters from those folks, and from Baha'i people and others. But the only really *ugly* mail I get is from sexually confused people. Mean letters come from unscriptural patriarchal nuts who automatically look down on women as a sex. The same ugliness arrives from the feminists who inveterately hate all things male. But the meanest notes of all come from members of the homosexual community who tell me in their letters that they are offended by the idea of men being scripturally expected to "act like men."

The sad reality is that once one gives in to the popular sexual confusion of our time, one loses focus. And because verse 14 flows out of verse 13, one eventually loses the capacity to love.

Adam Carolla's book *In Fifty Years We'll All Be Chicks* has a fine thesis; however, the text is ruined by continuous filth. I think Carolla misunderstands many aspect of manliness that we'll address in later chapters. That said, he's spot on when he addresses the issue of sexual confusion:

> For far too long I've stood idly by and watched a problem in this country get worse and worse. I'm talking about the [feminization] of America. We've become self-entitled, thin-skinned, hyperallergenic, gender-neutral little girls. What we used to settle with common sense or a fist we now settle with hand sanitizer and lawyers. I get labeled a misogynist all the time. But I'm simply pointing out that men and women are different ... As a culture we decided the smaller the chasm between male and female, the more

evolved our society would be. But truth is … we're *different* and that's a good thing. Why is it that the same people who beat the celebrate-differences drum when it comes to cultures refuse to acknowledge the biggest cultural difference on the planet? Men and women.[17]

That's exactly what Paul was saying to Corinth two thousand years ago. Act like men and let all you do be done in love. Some of you don't spend much time either in academia or popular culture, so you may not realize how serious and widespread sexual confusion has become. To help illustrate the depth of the problem for you, a member of our pulpit team (the lay group that evaluates my work and helps me craft these studies) forwarded this recent example to me.

The *Psychology of Women Quarterly* published an article about a study that found that when men act gentlemanly toward women both sexes experience increased life satisfaction.[18] "That's wonderful!" you declare. "We call that gentlemanliness in our home."

Not so fast. The authors conclude that this is incredibly dangerous behavior because it de facto promotes what the study calls "benevolent sexism." They write: "Our findings of increased life satisfaction reinforce the dangerous nature of benevolent sexism and emphasize the need for interventions to reduce its prevalence."[19]

The article continues, showing that these academics desire laws that make it illegal for a man to hold a door for a female. Such is the confusion that's screaming for your attention, friends. By the way, Charles Murray had the best response to the study's authors:

> When social scientists discover something that increases life satisfaction for both sexes, shouldn't they at least consider the possibility that they have come across something that is positive? Healthy? Something that might even conceivably be grounded in the nature of *Homo sapiens*?[20]

Gentlemanliness is grounded in our nature. That's why God tells us to act like men and do all in love! Gentlemanliness and femininity are part of how God created us as male and female. So keep your head clear of unisex confusion!

#3—If you want to remain strong-minded in truth, keep your head clear of shame.

Shame is merely a lie that God is limited. For the Christian, that's what shame really represents—a lie. If you want to stay useful to God you must remain focused on truth, not lies. Ken Gire addresses this in his book *Relentless Pursuit.* In chapter 4 of that book, Gire discusses the work by Brené Brown, a research professor at the University of Houston who wrote a book titled *The Hustle for Worthiness.*

She's done some really interesting work on the perils of the "performance trap"—trying to make your shame self-acceptable through what you do, instead of letting what you do flow from a thoroughly accepted self. After reading Brown's book and looking through Scripture, Gire writes this summary:

> Shame is a lynchpin lie. [Shame is] the "intensely painful feeling or experience of believing that we are flawed and therefore unworthy of love and belonging" … Put a makeup mirror to your face and turn on its fluorescent light. Look at the pores on your nose and the hairs in your nostrils. Focus on the wrinkles around your eyes and the gullies under them. Shame believes that this magnified face is your true face, the one everybody else—especially God—is focused on. Shame can isolate you, drive you away from community. Shame accuses you of being unworthy of love and belonging and joy. Shame can even blackmail you. If everyone knew the truth about you, they would see you for the fraud you are and wouldn't want to be around you … Shame corrodes the very part of us that believes we are capable of change.[21]

That's beautifully said. Shame takes our eyes off of God and His redemptive work and plants our attention firmly on ourselves. Instead of believing lies that you are unloved or unworthy, listen to Almighty God in Isaiah 46:3-4:

> "Listen to Me, house of Jacob,
> all the remnant of the house of Israel,
> who have been sustained from the womb,

carried along since birth.
I will be the same until your old age,
and I will bear you up when you turn gray.
I have made you, and I will carry you;
I will bear and save you. (HCSB)

This is also true for all Gentiles who have trusted in Jesus, the Jewish Messiah. Believing Gentiles are grafted into the promises given Abraham's offspring so that you are upheld by God's loving hand! "But," we ask in that small, fearful, child voice in our heads, "What about all my sins? What about the evil that is surely in my flesh?" Read with me, friends, and think on God's truth in Psalm 103:11-12:

For as high as the heavens
are above the earth,
So great is His lovingkindness
toward those who fear Him.
As far as the east
is from the west,
So far has He removed
our transgressions from us. (NASB)

Now think about Paul's parallel statement in Romans 8:1:

Therefore, no condemnation now exists for those in Christ Jesus … . (HCSB)

If you have trusted in Jesus as Savior, there is no condemnation for you. Yes, God loves you enough to spank and set you straight. God does use healthy communities to appropriately stigmatize bad behavior. Yet there is no *shame*. Shame is just a lie that gets your eyes off of truth and onto yourself.

STAY IN CONTROL (VS. 5).

Do you want to prosper spiritually? Want to win your important life wrestling matches? Then stay focused on truth and stay in control. That's the issue in the next verse of our 2 Timothy text:

> But you, be sober in all things, endure hardship, do the work
> of an evangelist, fulfill your ministry. (NASB)

There is so much richness to mine here! However, in order to stay focused on our topic, we'll just examine one key word—*nephro*. We translate *nephro* as "be sober"—and that's appropriate, since the term to Greeks indicated "freedom from intoxicants." Yet *nephro* means even more. *Nephro* is more than not being drunk; it implies the importance of being freed from outside control. Being sober means that one is not under any negative influence.

A big part of wrestling was getting into my opponent's head. Part of my job was to convince him that I was stronger, faster, and more controlling than he could handle. Then, worrying about me, that other wrestler could no longer focus on controlling himself. He couldn't pay attention to wrestling his match.

That's what intoxicants do in our lives. They eliminate our self-control. What are some intoxicants that can get people off base? There are many, but let's look at only two that are not discussed enough in church:

#1—If you want to exercise biblical self-control, you must keep your head clear of narcissisms.

Narcissism is infatuation with self. It is a lie that uses inbuilt human insecurity to inflate aspects of self. Humans have always struggled with narcissism. The Greeks gave us the term through their very ancient myth of Narcissus. And yet, we are rapidly becoming experts at Narcissism today. It's destroying our ability to be in control, especially of our emotions, work, and culture.

Consider this article from Dr. Keith Ablow, published by Fox News:

> A new analysis of the American Freshman Survey, which has
> accumulated data for the past 47 years from 9 million young
> adults, reveals that college students are more likely than ever
> to call themselves gifted and driven to succeed, even though
> their test scores and time spent studying are decreasing.

Psychologist Jean Twenge, the lead author of the analysis, is also the author of a study showing that the tendency toward narcissism in students is up 30 percent in the last thirty-odd years. This data is not unexpected. I have been writing a great deal over the past few years about the toxic psychological impact of media and technology on children, adolescents and young adults, particularly as it regards turning them into faux celebrities—the equivalent of lead actors in their own fictionalized life stories. ...

All the while, these adolescents, teens and young adults are watching a Congress that can't control its manic, euphoric, narcissistic spending, a president that can't see his way through to applauding genuine and extraordinary achievements in business, a society that blames mass killings on guns, not the psychotic people who wield them, and—here no surprise—a stock market that keeps rising and falling like a roller coaster as bubbles inflate and then, inevitably, burst.

That's really the unavoidable end, by the way. False pride can never be sustained. The bubble of narcissism is always at risk of bursting. That's why young people are higher on drugs than ever, drunker than ever, smoking more, tattooed more, pierced more and having more and more and more sex, earlier and earlier and earlier, raising babies before they can do it well, because these things make them feel special, for a while. They're doing anything to distract themselves from the fact that they feel empty inside and unworthy.

Distractions, however, are temporary, and the truth is eternal. Watch for an epidemic of depression and suicidality, not to mention homicidality, as the real self-loathing and hatred of others that lies beneath all this narcissism rises to the surface. I see it happening and, no doubt, many of you do, too.[22]

Such is the reality and the danger of narcissism, friends. It erodes self-control, which is really the core issue the doctor is discussing. Of course one of the most popular narcissisms—especially for males—is pornography. Porn is a self-centered lie that objectifies women. Females made in God's image and for whom He died are recast as mere objects.

Porn lies by pretending a man has no power to resist sin and exalts his measly self-image with narcissistic fantasy. And porn is an incredible eroder of self-control. I wish I had a dollar for every person I have heard cry about how they just can't keep away from those false images that call to them like Sirens. They know they are destroying their self-control—and their very lives—on the rocks. But they always steer the ship toward the Siren of porn anyway.

If you or someone you love is wrapped up in pornography, there is help. You can attack the basic narcissistic lie that drives your lack of self-control. Porn does not have to master you any longer. First, I highly recommend you read excellent books that detail the journeys of men whom God has guided out of the trap of pornography. *Samson of a Man* by Kevin McDowell is one that has been particularly useful.

Second, gain an active accountability helper. Call one of your local pastors. Grab a guy at your small group or Bible study or similar men's ministry. Go to lunch with him, confess your sin, and get some help getting back to humanity. Visit a licensed Christian therapist who specializes in sexual compulsions.

According to Genesis 3, the height of humanity is to resist temptation. Despite the sin that came to us from Adam, you and I can truly overcome temptation. By God's power and with our brethren, we can be in real control, lashed to the mast, rejecting the narcissism of porn.

#2—If you want to exercise biblical self-control keep your head clear of hurriedness.

This is a second intoxicant that goes underreported—hurriedness. Remember, we are to be sober-minded. There are times that any person will be busy, a condition that appears to be biblically fine. Jesus also lived through some exhaustingly busy days. But He was never hurried. He had a true north on His compass that could not be shaken. Jesus was always ready to step away; to go spend needed time alone with the Father; to maintain the spiritual fruit of self-control.[23]

By contrast, many medical, business, and political leaders exalt hurriedness. They praise the person who is hurried. The pretend that the person surrounded by hovering assistants and under constant time pressure is in control. Wise people know better. All that immediacy fills your life until you are the *slave*, not the master.

Being hurried is like shaving with a hatchet or hanging sandpaper on your toilet roller. It isn't manly; it's just stupid. Such nonsense doesn't make you tough; it just makes you idiotic. Same thing is true for inflated hurriedness. It doesn't mean you're cool. It means you are a slave. Further, hurriedness has an awful long-term effect. Hurried people lose the capacity to think. Being hurried erodes the ability to really think.

Again, there's nothing inherently evil about being busy—just as hatchets and sandpaper aren't evil—but when one misuses busyness to become hurried, then you have a problem. And frankly we are experts at misusing good things to make ourselves hurried. Television, your e-reader, video games, and various communication devices are all fine things. They are fine in the way that wine is fine. But like alcohol, they quickly and easily overwhelm. They enslave. They are addictive and take you away from the fulfilling self-control God desires for you.

STAY CONCENTRATED ON END RESULTS (VSS. 6-8).

Winning in life is about focus, and real men keep their focus. They stay centered on truth. They stay in control. They also stay concentrated on end results, something Paul describes in verses 6-8:

> For I am already being poured out as a drink offering, and the time of my departure has come. I have fought the good fight, I have finished the course, I have kept the faith; in the future there is laid up for me the crown of righteousness, which the Lord, the righteous Judge, will award to me on that day; and not only to me, but also to all who have loved His appearing. (NASB)

Notice the commitment to build on the work of others who have gone before us, to complete what God has called us to do, and then to faithfully exhort those whom God will bring next. "My time is ending, so you get after it." This is a long-term focus.

This is why short sellers on Wall Street make bad traders in the long run. They have no view for the long haul. This is why children who settle for candy houses get captured by the witch. This is why athletes who take steroids ultimately fail; why Dads who always scream to get their way ultimately lose; why Moms and Dads who give in to whiny children raise brats. Without long-term focus, there is no lasting victory. Unless you think things through to end results, you will lose.

Paul is writing about his own life and showing his protégé Timothy that long-term focus is key. Paul knows there are rewards in eternity because he lived his life in light of those rewards. He didn't live for short-term things on earth. What about us? Do we look to the end results? I got a letter from a young man who gets it. He is establishing his life on Paul's pattern, setting his focus on the finish line. Look what he wrote:

> I have the choice to remember that I am God's every day and that it is worth it to keep in mind the eternal rewards that lie ahead. It is when I do not run to the Word that I fall into slavery of this world. To remember I am God's leads me to consistent integrity in all my commitments. The only way I can finish strong is to remember daily Whose I am.[24]

Now, look at verses 9-11. Here we learn to stay attentive to pleasing God, not culture

> Make every effort to come to me soon; for Demas, having loved this present world, has deserted me and gone to Thessalonica; Crescens has gone to Galatia, Titus to Dalmatia. Only Luke is with me. Pick up Mark and bring him with you, for he is useful to me for service. (NASB)

Keep your focus God rather than the world!

STAY ATTENTIVE TO PLEASING GOD, NOT CULTURE (VSS. 9-11).

Once again we could spend years on these words, but we'll move quickly for our present purposes. Out of all these amazing characters, just look at Demas. Demas has deserted his redeemed community. He has abandoned his brethren because he loved this present world. That's why Paul wants Timothy and John Mark to come. Unlike Demas, they look to the long-term.

"Present world" is the Greek *nun aioona*. *Nun* means now. *Aion* is the word for an "age" or a "culture." Thus we see that Demas loved all the rewards of the present world culture. Now, before we wag our fingers at Demas, it's wise to try and understand his situation.

Demas lived in the Roman Empire. There was remarkable world-wide peace in his time. Trade was free and aggressive. Taxes were low. Life expectancy was seventy years. Women could own property, and divorce a husband or abort a child on demand. Cities were safe and clean. The first great shopping malls of the day were driving down prices and lifting profits.

The bottom line is that Demas was looking at a rather attractive world. No wonder he loved the rewards of the world culture and lost sight of the life to come. Sadly, the poor fool squandered his opportunity to be blessed in both worlds by choosing to focus on the wrong one. That was Jesus' point in Matthew 6:33:

> Seek first His [the Father's] kingdom and His righteousness; and all these things shall be added to you. (NASB)

Aren't you glad we always follow Jesus' instruction? Isn't it great that you and I are never like Demas! Or, are we?

Many of the people I teach are kind enough to connect with me via social media, and I spend some time every week reading their various posts. While most of them are funny and interesting, more than a few make me think that we're a lot more like Demas than we are like Jesus. We must honestly look in the mirror and confess our lack of proper focus. We are like Demas—more in love with the temporary culture than the eternal Lord.

If we want long-term victory, we must become more like Jesus … more like Daniel and his friends in Babylonian exile … more like William Wilberforce fighting popular slavery in England … more like Martin Luther King, Jr. fighting popular racism. That's my prayer when I peruse my life the posts of Facebook friends. It was also Paul's prayer for all Christians in Colossians 1:9-10:

> We haven't stopped praying for you. We are asking that you may be filled with the knowledge of His will in all wisdom and spiritual understanding, so that you may walk worthy of the Lord, fully pleasing to Him, bearing fruit in every good work and growing in the knowledge of God. (HCSB)

STAY COMMITTED TO SELF-SACRIFICING (VS. 12).

Paul also teaches us to stay committed to self-sacrificing. How does one keep one's focus? Please God, not culture. Read verse 12 in 2 Timothy 4:

> But Tychicus I have sent to Ephesus. (NASB)

Imagine sending a helper to others when you are in obvious need yourself. That's exactly what God's apostle did here. Remember, Paul was in prison when he wrote the letter and this second imprisonment of his was the type where he could survive only if he had outside support. Paul needed friends outside for everything, from food to companionship. Yet, he sends away Tychicus because he sees other people as more in need than is he. Real men and women—the people God really uses—are other-centered. They are self-sacrificing. It's a way we stay focused on truth.

A longtime friend of mine was producing a big music show a few years ago. He took me backstage to have supper with a bunch of the famous and popular artists. They were all really enjoyable folks and we had a great time. Later, I sat on a corner of the stage and watched 17,000 people go absolutely bonkers singing along during the concert.

I wish you could have seen it, especially the crowd response to the last song. MercyMe sang their signature hit "So Long Self." I could hardly hear the band! Those thousands of people were singing along so loudly that I could hardly hear the sound coming out of the band's monitors. It was wild! In response, I prayed for those worshippers what I pray for myself all the time: "Lord, may we really mean it when we sing along to those words."

May we truly die to self daily; pick up our crosses; yield to God's Spirit instead of the selfish inner self. May we truly sing "So long, self."

STAY IMMERSED IN THE SCRIPTURES (VS. 13).

Of course, the best way to stay focused on selflessnesst is to stay immersed in the Scriptures. That's the point in verse 13:

> When you come bring the cloak which I left at Troas with Carpus, and the books, especially the parchments. (NASB)

Paul wants the Scriptures. He also desires his coat, likely because it's cold in prison. The "books" could be Scripture or other writings. "Parchments" is a term a Hebrew like Paul would only have used of Scripture, which was always copied onto long-lasting animal-skin parchment scrolls. Even at his age, in his situation, Paul is keeping his mind fixed on the excellence of God's Word. If we wish to keep our heads together through trials, we must do the same.

STAY UN-CROTCHETY, EVEN IN CRISES (VSS.14-18).

Look now at how Paul wraps up this letter:

> Alexander the coppersmith did me much harm; the Lord will repay him according to his deeds. Be on guard against him yourself, for he vigorously opposed our teaching. At my first defense no one supported me, but all deserted me; may it not be counted against them. But the Lord stood with me, and strengthened me, in order that through me the proclamation might be fully accomplished, and that all the Gentiles might hear; and I was delivered out of the lion's mouth. The Lord will deliver me from every evil deed, and will bring me safely to His heavenly kingdom; to Him be the glory forever and ever. Amen. (NASB)

I am amazed at the way God's man handles this struggle. He does not give in to jaundiced cynicism, like most of us would. If we want to handle problems like he does—and we should—then we must stay un-crotchety, even in crises. God's people do not give in to grumpiness. Instead, they trust the Lord as did Paul.

Dennis Rainey wrote a wonderful book for men called *Stepping Up*. Near the end, Dennis is discussing the kind of trans-generational impact God wants people to have. Dennis calls this "being a patriarch," and he closes with this statement:

> As men grow old they've experienced enough disappoint-ment that they can easily become disillusioned, bitter, grum-bly, and cynical. [WB note: women are not immune to this, but men seem much more prone. There's a reason "grumpy old men" is a stereotype.] They can become crotchety old men. Listen: you can't be a patriarch and crotchety at the same time.[25]

Older people, Dennis is right. Just because you are older doesn't mean you have earned the right to lose focus! To finish well and complete the race as God desires we must remain yoked in to God's peace and call-ing all the way to the end. I was once blessed to hear a rather senior guy expound on the subject. My professor, Dr. Howard Hendricks, told me the following when he was eighty years young:

> You will never find me retiring onto some golf course far away from people who need to hear God's Word and see a man live it out. I may be old and only have one eye, but I am not going to hide away or become a grumpy old man. God has put fight in me and intends me to stay in the fight to the end.[26]

His point wasn't that retirement is evil. The point is that we are called to follow Jesus and keep our focus all the way to the end of the match.

CHAPTER 3

A REAL MAN SERVES AND LEADS

CHAPTER SUMMARY: The biblical ideal of manhood is a servant-leader. Men are called to be in-charge leaders who are continuously giving of self to empower those around them. Jesus is the consummate example of servant leadership, and His Word contains numerous examples of this and calls for men to grow as imitators of Him. In particular, men are called to exhibit biblical models of providers, husbands, and fathers.

LIFE CHANGE OBJECTIVE: That we serve and lead as God instructed and empowers.

RUNNING UPHILL WITH DAD

In his great book *Tender Warrior*, Stu Weber tells this fantastic story:

Down the hill from our house was a vacant lot. On one occasion Dad and I were down there together ... must have been playing catch, I don't remember. But I'll never forget the run up the hill.

In the midst of our activity, Mom came to the front porch of "old 3309" (an affectionate reference to our home) and called us to dinner. Dad and I glanced at each other. Our eyes met. They sparkled. Without a word we both sensed it was "time for a race." We took off. It was 150 yards uphill to the house. It was glorious running along with my Dad. Man, it was great! But try as I might, my little legs couldn't keep up with his long ones. He started to pull ahead. My neck strained. My muscles stretched. But I was losing ground. Then something really special happened.

Dad, seeing me start to drop back, reached out his hand to me. His eyes said, *Grab hold. Let's run together.*

Still running, my little hand slipped inside his larger one. It was like magic! His power lifted me right off the ground. I took off in his strength. My speed doubled because my dad had hold of me.

That's a lot like life. A kid's speed doubles when dad takes hold at home. *Take hold*, Dad! Hold on for all you're worth. Hold on in the face of storms and disappointments and sorrows and temptations and hurts and crazy, churning circumstances. There isn't much of anything in life children can't face with Dad's strong hand wrapped tightly around theirs.

And while you're at it, with your other hand, hold on tightly to your Heavenly Father's hand. Let Him be your confidence and wisdom and stability when you just can't find your own. Let His strength pull you up life's long hills until you can stand together, laughing and catching your breath, on heaven's front porch.

Isn't that what dads are for?[27]

Weber's book was written quite a few years ago, but I have never found a better example of what it means to be a servant-leader. And we must understand that servant-leadership—what Stu is describing—is God's ideal. It's how He leads us. That's why Jesus said this to His followers in Mark 9:33-35:

And they came to Capernaum; and when He was in the house, He began to question them, "What were you discussing on the way?" But they kept silent, for on the way they had discussed with one another which of them was the greatest. And sitting down, He called the twelve and said to them, "If anyone wants to be first, he shall be last of all, and servant of all." (NASB)

That's what God wants for each of us: to be servant-leaders. Weber has given us an image that helps us understand that big idea in a nutshell— the servant-leader has one hand pulling others along while the servant-leader's other hand is resting in the strengthening grip of the Father.

We're studying biblical manhood in this book, and we've come to an important point that applies to all Christians: the follower of Jesus serves and leads. Yes, this applies to guys and gals equally. However, we must be acutely concerned about a culture that doesn't understand this as it relates to males. In general, I think women in our day have proven more committed to the servant-leader ethic than have men.

Recently, a friend told me about his daughter and son-in-law's work in inner-city Dallas. They live in a rather rough apartment complex and build positive relationships with the boys who run loose around the area. Recently four pre-teen boys were in their apartment talking with the young couple. Somehow, fathering came up. The boys were utterly clueless about the concept that a Dad is supposed to be a servant-leader. Of course, their ignorance was understandable. Of those four boys, only one knew who was his father. He had no relationship with the man, but did at least know who he was and could indentify him. The others had no idea. That started a conversation about all of their friends. It turns out that among all their buddies in their school class, that one boy is the *only* one who knows the name of his father.

We live in a time and place where a generation is growing up clueless about the servant-leadership expected in men. They are struggling up a hill with no hand to hold, and are thus in real danger of not knowing how to hold their own hand out for others coming behind them. Thankfully, God is the father to the fatherless. And God expects us to take his Scripture and address this appalling lack of masculine servant leadership. Therefore, you and I are going to address the problem in our own hearts and then let our change lead to transformation in the world around us.

THE SERVANT-LEADER AND HIS PROVISION

We should start with possibly the most misunderstood concept about servant-leadership as it relates to men: The servant-leader and his provision. Provision is not what the world tries to make it. It's not some cultural role where a guy has to earn all the money. Read that again. There is *nothing* in the Bible that says that a male has to provide for his family.

HE RECOGNIZES GOD AS THE PROVIDER (1 TIMOTHY 6:17)

God provides; that isn't anyone else's job. We literally could turn to hundreds of texts to support this, but let's read 1 Timothy 6:17:

> Instruct those who are rich in the present age not to be arrogant or to set their hope on the uncertainty of wealth, but on God, who richly provides us with all things to enjoy. (HCSB)

According to God's Word, who provides? He does. Period. And we mustn't forget it. The servant leader recognizes God as the Provider. Our culture forgets it. Human nature screams out, "It's my money, and I earned it!" But it's not your money. It's a gift from God. The Provider is far greater and more generous than you could ever be if you were the real provider. That's one reason our Puritan forefathers often referred to God as "Providence." He is the One and only true Provider.

I read lots of books and articles every year. Sadly, most of the stuff I read about men has this tragic flaw: it's written as if 1950s TV shows are Scripture. There is nothing in the Bible about the guy going off to work 8-5 and the wife wearing pearls as she cleans house. That may be fine, but it's not Scripture! Almost all books on men's ministry have this fatal flaw—they act as if it's up to the dude to provide. It's not. That is God's job; and any time you try to fill God's shoes you are in for failure.

Men's ministry leaders usually get angry whenever I mention that it's not the man's job to provide. After all, no one likes being knocked off the throne of God, even if they don't belong there. But we don't belong there. And for the good of the kingdom, we need to stop playing like we're God.

Of course there is a valid question that often gets asked in response, "OK, so the servant-leader doesn't carry the burden of being the Provider. Granted. But what then does he do? Besides recognizing the Lord, what *does* God desire the servant-leader to do?" Great question! Look at the biblical text of Genesis 2. The answer begins in verse 15:

> Then the LORD God took the man and put him into the garden of Eden to cultivate it and keep it. (NASB)

The answer is right there.

HE WORKS FOR THE LORD (GENESIS 2:15).

That's what the servant-leader has been expected to do from the beginning. You and I are commanded to work! It's part of how God made people. Work even came before sin entered the world. And whatever one's career, our vocation is biblically clear: we work unto the Lord. That's the brilliant and beautifully-stated point in Colossians 3:23-24:

> Whatever you do, do it enthusiastically, as something done for the Lord and not for men, knowing that you will receive the reward of an inheritance from the Lord. You serve the Lord Christ. (HCSB)

God provides, but He lets servant-leaders partner with Him through work. Work is not how we provide for ourselves or for others. God does that. Work is how we join Him in His great ministry of provision.

Have you ever wondered why the Puritans, who had the strongest work ethic in history, were the ones to refer to God as "Providence?" Because they understood! We work, but it's all by God's grace because He is the Provider who gives us the strength to get up the hill. All comes from the Lord: every breath we take, every ounce of energy for work, even the strength to hold a hand out to the one following behind.

HE SCOUTS AND PLANS AHEAD (NUMBERS 13:25-30).

Now let's read from Numbers 13 and examine another aspect of the servant-leader and his provision. We read in Numbers 13:25-30:

> When they returned from spying out the land, at the end of forty days, they proceeded to come to Moses and Aaron and to all the congregation of the sons of Israel in the wilderness of Paran, at Kadesh; and they brought back word to them and to all the congregation and showed them the fruit of the land. Thus they told him, and said, "We went in to the land where you sent us; and it certainly does flow with milk and honey, and this is its fruit. Nevertheless, the people who live in the land are strong, and the cities are fortified and very large; and moreover, we saw the descendants of Anak there. Amalek is living in the land of the Negev and the Hittites and the Jebusites and the Amorites are living in the hill country, and the Canaanites are living by the sea and by the side of the Jordan." Then Caleb quieted the people before Moses, and said, "We should by all means go up and take possession of it, for we shall surely overcome it." (NASB)

The servant-leader scouts and plans ahead. This passage shows realism at its finest. These twelve men were sent out as scouts to find out the situation in the Promised Land God had granted Israel. Of course, one may wonder why scouts were sent at all. After all, God promised to give Israel the land if they would trust Him. So why didn't they just head on in? Why did the Lord command them to send an advance party?

I think God sent the spies ahead because of the partnership inherent in His provision. The battle belongs to the Lord, but He calls on His soldiers to fight. God is the provider, but He expects His people to work. Thus, a realistic assessment is important for people who are going to trust God as they go about His calling to fight. Somebody needs to always be scouting ahead. That's why it's so important to have point people like Caleb. They are the tip of the spear. They are the perfect pictures of what God expects from His servant-leaders—somebody who rises above all the mundane and looks ahead.

J. R. R. Tolkien's *The Hobbit* has a great picture of this. At one point in the story, Bilbo Baggins and his dwarf companions are lost in the impenetrable fastness of the great forest Mirkwood. And little Bilbo—in a turning point of his life—agrees to climb a great tree to get a perspective of where they are and whence they need to go. It's one of the bold choices that changes Bilbo and forms him into his true purpose as a servant-leader.

That's our purpose too! So what makes for a good point man? What is the most important trait in a scout? The answer seems to have everything to do with vision. When the scout, the point-man, has good vision, then the people in the wagon train can relax. The scout will know when floods or box canyons or hostiles are ahead, and the point man will give them ample warning. He will know what to do and when to do it.

But when you have a myopic scout, look out! Solomon knew that of which he spoke in Proverbs 29:18:

Where there is no vision, the people perish. (KJV)

Max Lucado provides a great commentary on that verse and our Numbers passage:

> Pilgrims with no vision of the promised land become proprietors of their own land ... Instead of looking upward at [the Lord], they look inward at themselves and outward at each other. The result? Cabin fever. Quarreling families. Restless leaders. Fence building. Staked-off territory. No trespassing! signs hung on hearts and homes. Spats turn into fights as myopic groups turn to glare at each other's weaknesses instead of turning to worship their common Strength.[28]

Men, if that describes your family or your ministry or your workplace, the problem is likely that you have stopped looking and planning ahead. Yes, females are servant-leaders as well. But guys have particular God-given roles that demand a man look ahead for the good of the whole company.

So what keeps us from doing so? Particularly, what keeps men from being bold scouts who are always looking ahead for the good of the team, the family, the country, the church? Why are great point men so rare? In my practice, reading, and travel I hear two reasons repeated *ad nauseum:*

#1—Reticence because of cultural anti-male bias is the number one thing I hear. A guy is afraid to step out and plan. He's concerned about leading ahead because he fears he'll come off like an ogre. Dudes today carry a heavy societal burden. If he's under the age of fifty and white, a man has been browbeaten all his life. He's had it beaten into his brain that he is *de jure* an oppressor.

Wives, your husband may be so scared of being an overbearing ogre that he naturally will cow to your leadership. Don't let him. Just pray for him and keep quiet. Don't grab the reigns of the scout horse. Be patient. And when the dude does lead, do not object. Don't call him a pushy ogre. Just say, "Lead on."

I'm not suggesting that you stop interacting as life partners. That's silly. You are equals in your marriage, bound together with the Lord. I am suggesting that you remember and support his role of point man; that you let him act as the primary scout for your family. You might also take into account that the modern Western man has been culturally indoctrinated to never trust masculine leadership, not even his own, so he likely needs a little support.

#2—The second reason guys don't scout ahead is that they settle for too little. The husband/father our society applauds is submissive, usually wrong, and absorbed only in his little world. He retreats to his man cave and has little influence in setting the agenda for his home.

Erma Bombeck was a funny voice of the 20th century, and I read lots of her stuff. In one of her last books, *Family—the Ties That Bind ... and Gag,* she wrote one of the saddest things I have ever read:

> One morning my father didn't get up and go to work. He went to the hospital and died the next day. I hadn't thought that much about him before. He was just someone who left and came home and seemed glad to see everyone. He opened the jar of pickles when no one else could. He was the only one in our house who wasn't afraid to go into the

basement by himself. Whenever I played house, the mother doll had a lot to do. I never knew what to do with the daddy doll, so I had him say, "I'm going off to work now"; and I put him under the bed.

The funeral was in our living room, and a lot of people came and brought all kinds of good food and cakes. We never had so much company before. I went to my room and felt under the bed for the daddy doll, and when I found him, I dusted him off and put him on my bed. He never did anything. I didn't know his leaving would hurt so much.[29]

Erma's daddy was a very good provider in the world's warped sense. They were wealthy. But according to his daughter's experience and according to Scripture, he settled for too little. He was only focused on worldly things. There were no goals of a spiritual or developmental nature in his home. And when he passed, his daughter could only say, "He never did anything."

HE INFUSES COURAGE ACCORDING TO GOD'S WORD (NUMBERS 13:30; JOSHUA 1:5-7).

Please look again at Numbers 13:30:

Then Caleb quieted the people before Moses, and said, "We should by all means go up and take possession of it, for we shall surely overcome it." (NASB)

If God provides, then what is the servant-leader meant to do? He works for the Lord; he scouts and plans ahead; and he infuses courage according to God's Word. You possibly know what occurs next in the story. The Israelites don't listen to God, Moses, Joshua, and Caleb. They rebel, and it costs an entire generation. But Joshua and Caleb, our stalwart scouts, learned that courage is critical. From that day at Kadesh on, their lives become long, awesome tales of courage.

Joshua definitely taught and infused courage. He gave out the same courage God infused into him. Let's flip a couple of books east in the Bible to Joshua 1. Reading this chapter, one can almost see the Father's hand helping Joshua up the hill. Hone in on Joshua 1:5-7.

No man will be able to stand before you all the days of your life. Just as I have been with Moses, I will be with you; I will not fail you or forsake you. Be strong and courageous, for you shall give this people possession of the land which I swore to their fathers to give them. Only be strong and very courageous; be careful to do according to all the law which Moses My servant commanded you; do not turn from it to the right or to the left, so that you may have success wherever you go. (NASB)

God encourages Joshua and teaches him to infuse that same strength into the people of Israel. The servant-leader encourages. That is, he makes people courageous.

I was blessed with a mom and dad who fired courage in me. They built me up. They kicked my bottom. They spurred me on. But in our current time, I see very little courage infusion. I see lots of helicopter parents making excuses for spoiled brats. I see lots of fathers who aren't in the picture. I see abandonments and bailouts on a national and family level. But I see very little courage.

The movie *Courageous* (2011) was specifically written and directed to address this issue. The film was a big hit—not because it was exceptionally well done, but because the message resonated with a country desperate for men to stand up and infuse courage. I highly recommend the film, and think there are a number of scenes that directly relate to this chapter of our study. Men, if you are going to be the servant-leaders you are designed to be, then you must be encouragers. Other biblical verses show this applies to gals as well. God's people are to be encouragers, not enablers.

THE SERVANT-LEADER AND HIS HUSBANDRY

Let's discuss the servant-leader and his husbandry. Both sexes are called to be servant-leaders, but only a man is called to be the husband. So what makes for good husbandry? The Bible actually has a lot to say about this, but I think we can fairly summarize it in two statements.

HE SEES HIMSELF AS HIS WIFE'S POSSESSION (1 CORINTHIANS 7:3-4).

#1—The husband is a servant-leader who sees himself as his wife's possession. 1 Corinthians 7 puts it pithily:

> Let the husband fulfill his duty to his wife, and likewise also the wife to her husband. The wife does not have authority over her own body, but the husband does; and likewise also the husband does not have authority over his own body, but the wife does. (NASB)

Gents, I have a news flash for you. If you are married, you are not your own. You belong to someone else. Your life is not your own. There is no part of it that is yours alone. A chemist would put it this way: you are not a free radical. You are bonded in a covalent bond. A godly man is unified with his other half in the Lord.

Men, one of the most heartbreaking things you can do is think and act as if you are a solo. Making decisions or purchases—even little ones—without thinking of the impact on your sweetheart is frankly unscriptural. Your life, your choices, are not your own. You belong in a permanent partnership. And of course, ladies, the text is clearly applied to you as well. In fact, this principle applies to all people, not merely those who are married. A few paragraphs earlier in this Corinthian letter, we read in 1 Corinthians 6:19b-20:

> Or do you not know that your body is a temple of the Holy Spirit who is in you, whom you have from God, and that you are not your own? For you have been bought with a price: therefore glorify God in your body. (NASB)

The wise person who wants to fulfill our servant-leader calling by running uphill holding God's hand remembers this: we are not our own. We operate in a permanent, wonderful, family relationship.

In the 1800s James Fennimore Cooper wrote the *Leatherstocking Tales*, five novels about life on the frontier and some of the first best-sellers in American history. Cooper developed many memorable characters, but none more awesome than Uncas, the last of the Mohicans. There may be no character in history who better exemplifies the idea of belonging to another. Uncas sees himself as belonging to his tribe, the great Delaware warriors who have gone before him. He sees himself as tied forever to Cora, the woman he rescues, protects, and loves. And Uncas sees himself as completely belonging to Jesus, in whom he trusts.

David Simmonds, a member of our pulpit team, wrote me about Uncas and 1 Corinthians. David said:

> I want to be like Uncas. I know Kelly [his wife] wants me to be that man. I am not talking about the tall, great hair and good looking part. No, I am talking about the 'I don't care what it takes, I will do anything and everything to find you. To not eat until you are safe. To not rest until you are in my arms. To always know that we are one.' I know God is like that with me. He wants me to know that He unites me with Him; and knowing that, I will not give in. I will fight and live for Him.[30]

David has it exactly right! His attitude is a great example and application of Paul's words in 1 Corinthains 6.

HE'S A ONE-WOMAN KIND OF MAN (1 TIMOTHY 3:1-2).
Here's the second great truth about husbandry:

#2—The servant-leader is a one-woman kind of man. He is his wife's possession and he's a one-woman kind of man. Mull over God's instruction in the first two verses of 1 Timothy 3:

> It is a trustworthy statement: if any man aspires to the office of overseer, it is a fine work he desires to do. An overseer, then, must be above reproach, the husband of one wife .... (NASB)

This passage presents the character qualities of elders in the local church. Gene Getz seems correct in his book *The Measure of a Man* when he discusses this passage. Dr. Getz contends that these traits should be seen in every man. The best character for the best is the best character for all. And the best character for all men is to be a one-woman kind of man.[31]

That's really what the Greek text says. *Einai miás gunaikós andra* translates "exist as one-woman man." The big issue isn't whether one is married or not nor how many times one has been wed. The bar in the text is much higher. It asks, "Are you a monogamous-minded person?" We already discussed faithfulness in this book, but here's another reminder. A godly man has sex with his wife and only his own wife. Moreover, he is only allows himself to think and act as a person in a closed relationship with God and his wife. He is the opposite of a flirting free radical. He is singular in focus.

Unmarried ladies, have you thought this trait through? You need to. Look, if he's not a faithful man before you are married, what reason is there to think he will become one afterwards? If he is willing to sleep with you out of wedlock, why wouldn't he be willing to do the same later with someone else?

It's really sad. The statistics are clear in study after study: married monogamous people who stay wed and monogamous for twenty or more years have by far the most satisfying sex of any group. Just look at the Family Research Council summary of twenty years' worth of research on sexual satisfaction[32]:

Overall Sexual Satisfaction

40%
Married, unfaithful

43%
Unmarried

83%
Married, faithful less than 20 yrs

92%
Married, faithful more than 20 yrs

The numbers on the chart are very telling. And yet, we live in a world where every single TV show, movie, and book screams the opposite. They lie. They say that sex in the city is the real way to happiness.

Ridiculous! One-woman men and one-man women are the shining gold standard. Everything else is just shades of grey.

For those of you who are raising boys, Robert Lewis does a great job developing this theme in his book *Raising A Modern-Day Knight*. Robert says that a man's code of conduct is guided by four principles, all of which he supports from Scripture: a will to obey, a work to do, one woman to love, and a transcendent cause.[33] I recommend it as a practical guide to building up one-woman men in a fifty shades of grey world.

Speaking of a transcendent cause, I got another great note on this from Randall Satchell of our pulpit team.

> Wayne, in the section on husbandry don't forget the single guys. A single man, whether young or old, is to still be a servant-leader. His "wife" is the Church, and his care is for the things of the Lord.[34]

He is right! That's why a few lines later, 1 Corinthians 7:32 makes a powerful statement about the primacy of connection to Christ:

> One who is unmarried is concerned about the things of the Lord, how he may please the Lord. (NASB)

THE SERVANT-LEADER AND HIS FATHERING

Remember those lost boys in the inner-city apartment? The glaring hole in their lives was a lack of a human father. So let's discuss the servant-leader and his fathering. Again, the Bible has much to say about this but I have attempted to reduce the copious biblical information on this topic to two summary truths:

HE ACTIVELY TEACHES HIS CHILDREN TRUTH (PSALM 78:5-7).

#1—He actively teaches his children truth.

As one among many choices, let's read Psalm 78:5-7. As originally written, this song is broken into pieces almost surely meant to be read responsively line by line, but in this format we'll just have to imagine the descant of each other's voices. The psalmist writes of God:

> He established a rule in Jacob;
> he set up a law in Israel.
> He commanded our ancestors
> to make his deeds known to their descendants,
> so that the next generation, children yet to be born,
> might know about them.
> They will grow up and tell their descendants about them.
> Then they will place their confidence in God.
> They will not forget the works of God,
> and they will obey his commands. (NET)

Deuteronomy 6 speaks to the same idea, emphasizing that this is a partnership among a man, his wife, and the entire redeemed community. Later, the book of Hebrews addresses the discipline and correction aspects of this. The bottom line throughout is that the father is biblically charged with teaching his children the most important truths of life.

Unfortunately, most young people today have that role fulfilled by television, friends, and a sometimes-misguided school system. If a father is involved, it's something along the lines of a cartoonish, buffoonish sit-com. That is not the way to do it. Instead, here are some practical suggestions for fulfilling your calling to be the active teacher of your children:

- At every age, discuss with your kids about important things like God, sex, family, friends. Don't save things up. Age-appropriately, cover all the big stuff again and again at each age.

After all, that's how you learned in school! For example, you likely studied the American Revolution in 2nd grade, 5th grade, 8th grade, and 10th grade—each time adding more layers of knowledge, but always building on the same foundation. Teach your kids life lessons the same way!

- Do not accept meetings on nights when you expect your kids to have lots of homework.

I don't! There are lessons that come up during that drudgery and I am going to be there for them! I'm not there merely to help with homework, but to grab those teachable moments that arise.

Regardless of how much your work makes you travel, we live in a time when you can easily keep up with the kids. You must, if you wish to father like the servant-leader God made you to be. Regardless of how removed or estranged your children are from you, you can and must fulfill your calling. Despite any distance, you can still write them, teach them, and encourage them in the most critical truths.

I know one father who made lunches for his kids every day for the seventeen years they had children in school. And every day he put in a brief note in of Scripture and an encouraging word. The notes became a sensation. Their kids' lunch friends wanted to read the notes in early elementary school. Then the kids began to laugh at the notes in late elementary and middle school. Yet by 9th grade, all their friends again looked forward to those notes. By high school, this one father's instruction actually spread to dozens of kids, who hung on his words every day.

- Above all else, you and I must bring our children to church, showing humble, receptive hearts ourselves.

Children can tell when something is just rote. And they can also tell when we are willing and excited learners ourselves. Children will model what we show excites us.

HE LEADS HIS FAMILY TO ENJOY THE LORD (JOSHUA 24:14-15).

The servant-leader fathers well by actively teaching truth to his kids. And,

#2—He leads his family to enjoy the Lord.

If we move to the end of the book of Joshua, in chapter 24:14-15, we find where the aged Joshua gives his final speech:

> "Now, therefore, fear the LORD and serve Him in sincerity and truth; and put away the gods which your fathers served beyond the River and in Egypt, and serve the LORD. And if it is disagreeable in your sight to serve the LORD, choose for yourselves today whom you will serve: whether the gods which your fathers served which were beyond the River, or the gods of the Amorites in whose land you are living; but as for me and my house, we will serve the LORD." (NASB)

Joshua knew his legacy. He had led his family to serve the Lord God alone. Whatever bumps or missteps they might face along the way, he was confident of the final outcome, because that was how he established the home.

Back in 2012, Michael Craven wrote a great column on this topic:

> The lack of actively involved fathers has produced societal conditions necessary for the intervention of government. It is a sobering fact when the government is compelled to respond to the failure of such a fundamental institution as family! Beginning in 2001, the U.S. Department of Health & Human Services under President Bush launched its *Fatherhood Initiative* with the following statement: "The President is determined to make committed, responsible fatherhood a national priority ... [T]he presence of two committed, involved parents contributes directly to better school performance, reduced substance abuse, less crime and delinquency, fewer emotional and other behavioral problems, less risk of abuse or neglect, and lower risk of teen suicide. The research is clear: fathers factor significantly in the lives of their children. There is simply no substitute for the love, involvement, and commitment of a responsible father.[35]

Dads have a great opportunity lead their family to enjoy the Lord. When they do so, all of society benefits. Ron Mo, the head of men's ministry at the church where I serve, shared some interesting research with the guys at one of our men's breakfasts and it is well worth considering. A rather obscure but large and important study conducted by the Swiss government in 1994 and published in 2000 revealed some astonishing facts with regard to the generational transmission of faith and religious values. The study abstract states in part: *"It is the religious practice of the father of the family that, above all, determines the future attendance at or absence from church of the children."*[36]

> Wow! Ron went on to share these specific findings from the research:
>
> If both father and mother attend regularly, 33 percent of their children will end up as regular churchgoers, and 41 percent will end up attending irregularly. *Only 25 percent of their children will end up not practicing at all.*
>
> If the father is irregular and mother regular, only 3 percent of the children will subsequently become regulars themselves, while a further 59 percent will become irregulars. *38 percent will be lost to church.*
>
> If the father is non-practicing but mother regular, only 2 percent of children will become regular worshippers, and 37 percent will attend irregularly. *Over 60 percent of their children will be lost completely to the church.*[37]

Now, consider the other possibilities. What happens if the father is regular but the mother irregular or non-practicing? Amazingly, the percentage of children becoming regular goes up to 38 percent with the irregular mother and up to 44 percent with the non-practicing. The authors conclude that this suggests that "loyalty to the father's commitment *grows* in response to the mother's laxity or indifference to religion."[38]

Ron concluded, "In short, if a father does not go to church—no matter how faithful his wife's devotions—only one child in 50 will become a regular worshipper. If a father does go regularly, regardless of the practice of the mother, between two-thirds and three-quarters of their children will become churchgoers (regular and irregular)."

Here's one final quote I grabbed from the research:

One of the reasons suggested for this distinction is that children tend to take their cues about domestic life from the mother while their conceptions of the world outside come from the father. If the father takes faith in God seriously then the message to their children is that God *should* be taken seriously.[39]

Friend, do you believe God should be taken seriously? If so, then, we have work to do. We need to live out our calling as servant-leaders. I know it's hard. It often feels like an uphill run. But your Heavenly Father is guiding you. He is encouraging you with all the strength needed to be courageous and to pass that strength on to those behind you.

CHAPTER 4

A REAL MAN
FIGHTS FOR RIGHT

CHAPTER SUMMARY: Today, the idea of standing for right seems laughable to many. Our culture awash with relativism questions whether "right" is knowable. Men trained to be selfish children in thought look to their own pleasure and never consider standing up to evil. The few visible warriors for good tend to be female, laudable, but also lamentable by the absence of male voices. Men have remained boys, leaving a cultural vacuum that is eroding our culture. The solution is a return to the great images of manhood in Scripture: the warrior and the kinsman-redeemer.

LIFE CHANGE OBJECTIVE: That we "man up."

Kay Hymnowitz wrote a book, *Manning Up: How the Rise of Women Has Turned Men into Boys.* Though I disagree with some of the book, it does an excellent job of exposing a huge problem. Here's a sample:

> "Jersey Shore" is the extreme manifestation of the if-it-feels-good-do-it, nothing sacred, girls-like-it-as-much-as-boys, post-'60s America. Recently, I happened to turn on an episode of "Jersey Shore." It was the one where Deena's sister goes out with Mike's brother and does

something so sexually audacious—I'm a little vague on the details—that Mike can't stop talking about it. Then Deena gives Mike a piece of her mind for spreading rumors about her sister, and then Mike tells Deena that, hold on a minute, he thinks her sister is the bomb for whatever unmentionable thing she did.[40]

Ms. Hymnowitz does a great job exposing how the "Jersey Shore" mentality works. The current culture positions the dude to get all he wants with no commitment. The females are willing accessories to this, having entered a sacred social pact that prohibits them from expecting any male to act grown up and do the right thing. Hymnowitz continues:

Thanks to the sexual revolution ... and the 1973 ruling in Roe v. Wade legalizing abortion as a backup plan ... many women feel that the old social pressure to avoid premarital sex has been replaced with pressure to just do it. Many privately complain about the disappearance of the gentlemanly arts. The results are telling:

Today a record 41% of children are born to single mothers; most of those mothers are low-income women in their early and mid-20s. Since single motherhood tends to depress education rates and wages, poor mothers are at greater risk of staying that way and reducing their children's life chances ... It isn't going too far to say that the sexual revolution has helped to increase poverty and inequality.

The prevalence of "multi-partner fertility"—women having successive children by different men and men successive children by different women—has added to the disorder of many American neighborhoods. "Unintended" pregnancies, repeat abortions, sexually transmitted diseases, multi-partner fertility, single motherhood, not to mention feckless men: It sounds like a dystopia.[41]

Here's my one-sentence summary of Hymnowitz's thesis:

Men have remained boys, leaving a cultural vacuum that is sucking the life out of America.

I will boldly tell you that God has the solution for our cultural dystopia. And the solution is biblical manhood.

But there's a problem with accessing God's solution. There may be nothing in the world today as poorly understood as real manhood. The closest most can come is the nebulous, slightly-funny-but-actually-sad idea of a "man card"—an imaginary card that certifies males to be men. (If you are unfamiliar with the idea, you can read all about it online at sites like urbandictionary.com!) "Man cards" come nowhere close to the inner power and majesty of biblical manhood. Biblical manhood is not lowest-common denominator cultural maleness. Things like belching, sports, grilling, basso profundo vocal range are complete non-issues in the real make-up of a man.

The Scripture deals with real masculinity. But sadly, our culture—and even our church culture—is more concerned with the shallow flippancies of a "man card." Instead of taking our cues from "Jersey Shore" or Man Card, let's get our direction from God. And the Lord tells us this in 1 Corinthians 16:13:

Be watchful, stand firm in the faith, act like men, be strong.
Let all that you do be done in love. (ESV)

THE BIBLICAL MAN IS A KINSMAN-REDEEMER.

So what does it mean to "act like a man?" The Bible gives two big answers to that great question:

#1—The biblical man is a kinsman-redeemer. One of the great types running through the Bible is the kinsman-redeemer. Dallas Theological Seminary professor Stephen Braemer gives an excellent summary: "The kinsman-redeemer is a male relative who, according to various laws found in the Pentateuch [books of Moses], had the privilege or responsibility to act for a relative who was in trouble, danger, or need of vindication."[42]

The original Hebrew verb *ga-al* or *go-el* is the root of the idea. And it appears more than a hundred times in the Old Testament. *Ga-al* is kinsman, a relative, a redeemer or vindicator who stands for the family member in need. And it's a really old idea. One of the oldest books ever penned—Job—concerns itself with the kinsman-redeemer. In fact, Job gives a cool twist to the whole idea, claiming in chapter 19 verse 25 that God Himself is Job's kinsman-redeemer:

> And as for me, I know that my Redeemer *(Ga-al)* lives. (NASB)

In context, Job is talking about God Almighty. God is Himself *Ga-al* to Job. The Old Testament will build on this, describing God as the rescuer of His people, their kinsman-redeemer. The New Testament rounds out the idea beautifully, as Dr. Braemer explains:

> Christ can be regarded as an example of a kinsman-redeemer since he identified himself with us and redeemed us because of our need. Hebrews 2:11 states that "Both the one who makes men holy and those who are made holy are of the same family. So Jesus is not ashamed to call them brothers." Jesus is not only our redeemer from sin, but as Hebrews 2 goes on to point out, he is a kinsman to us and understands our struggles. Thus he is able to help us in our times of need.[43]

Now, the rest of the Scriptures go on to describe that because we are rescued by our kinsman-redeemer, He expects us to become kinsman-redeemers ourselves. We are supposed to start looking like and living like Jesus, the older brother we adore. Colossians 3:10 describes this process:

> … put on the new self who is being renewed to a true knowledge according to the image of the One who created him. (NASB)

God is the related one who loves humans enough to redeem them. He does not do this because it's fair or because people deserve it. He does this because of Who He is, the God of love and mercy who becomes kinsman in order to redeem people. Because Christians are being remade in His own image, it follows that we are to become redeeming people of love and mercy ourselves. That is true manhood. This is why Paul said in 1 Corinthians for all to be done in love.

THE KINSMAN-REDEEMER IS A POWERFUL MAN OF FORCE.

In Ruth 2:1, we read that the kinsman-redeemer is a powerful man of force:

> Now Naomi had a kinsman of her husband, a man of great wealth, of the family of Elimelech, whose name was Boaz. (NASB)

And thus we meet Boaz. This is one of the noblest men in history— Boaz, the eventual husband of Ruth and grandsire of David. The key descriptor is right there in the middle. Look at the HCSB rendering of the verse.

> Now Naomi had a relative on her husband's side named Boaz. He was a prominent man of noble character from Elimelech's family. (HCSB)

"Prominent man of noble character" is the Hebrew *gibowr chayil*. As we noted in Chapter 1, this is literally "a powerful force." *Chayil* was often used of wealth, and it was also used to depict political power, but *chayil* is more than that. The text is telling us that Boaz is a powerful man of force. The meaning is not really physical, but instead describes all the non-material aspects of life. When ladies teach the book of Ruth, all tend to focus on Boaz's softness and kindness—and those things are important. But they must be seen in the context of *gibowr chayil*. This is a powerful, forceful man; a person with a strong soul.

Think it through. One can't really do any redeeming unless one has some power. Unless you have financial power, you can't help anyone in monetary need. Unless you have built political, economic, and moral strength, you cannot really do much rescuing. Unless you've developed wisdom, you can't really guide a lost soul well. Just as a physical weakling can't help hold up someone who's falling, so an immaterial weakling can't redeem effectively. Real men are kinsman-redeemers. And if you want to be a real man, you must develop your *gibowr chayil* and develop it for good.

This is why boys need supervision in their development. Boys do not grow into men of positive force without continual shaping. Dr. James Dobson addressed this in his book, *Bringing Up Boys*:

> Boys are like fast-moving automobiles that need a driver at the steering wheel every moment of the journey, gently turning a half inch here and a quarter inch there. They will need this guidance for at least sixteen or eighteen years, or even longer. When left to their own devices, they tend to drift toward the center divider or into the ditch, toward misbehavior or danger. Yet 59 percent of today's kids come home to an empty house after school each day. It is an invitation to disaster for rambunctious males, and the older they get, the more opportunities they have to get into trouble. Today, when the culture is in a tug-of-war with families for control of our children, we can't afford to be preoccupied with things of lesser consequence. Your task as a mother or father is to build a man out of the raw materials available implicitly in your delightful little boy. Construct him stone upon stone and precept upon precept. Never assume for a moment that you can go off and "do your own thing" without serious consequences for him and his sister.[44]

Power can be and must be developed and used for good. Jesus—the One in whose likeness we are being shaped—Jesus showed such power. John 18:1-6 records a very important moment from the night of Jesus' arrest. John writes:

> After saying these things, Jesus crossed the Kidron Valley with his disciples and entered a grove of olive trees. Judas, the betrayer, knew this place, because Jesus had gone there many times with his disciples. The leading priests and Pharisees had given Judas a battalion of Roman soldiers and Temple guards to accompany him. Now with blazing torches, lanterns, and weapons, they arrived at the olive

grove. Jesus fully realized all that was going to happen to him. Stepping forward to meet them, he asked, "Whom are you looking for?" "Jesus of Nazareth," they replied. "I am he," Jesus said. Judas was standing there with them when Jesus identified himself. And as he said, "I am he," they all fell backward to the ground! Once more he asked them, "Whom are you searching for?" And again they replied, "Jesus of Nazareth." (NLT)

I think that last sentence was probably spoken with a tremulous frightened squeak: "Jesus … of Nazareth?" Once when I was teaching in the Garden of Gethsemane, I read the text just like that. Then, I taught about Jesus' power. I taught that the kinsman-redeemer is a man of force and power developed and used for good. I declared that Jesus' self-sacrifice only makes sense in the context that He could knock an army on its bottoms with His word.

While I taught, an old gardener—an Israeli man who was working in the garden—was listening in. When I finished, he leaned on his hoe, looked me in the eye, and said, "That's right. You taught that rightly. Well done, son." And then he pottered away. Our whole group was stunned. We were speechless. Two ideas froze us on the spot. First, it felt like one of those events the book of Hebrews describes, where you entertain an angel in human form. Second, that old gardener exemplified exactly what we'd been discussing. He had a moral force that moved our whole group. And he used it to encourage me.

THE KINSMAN-REDEEMER STANDS UP FOR HIS PEOPLE.

Look again at the awesomeness of Boaz. Read from Ruth chapter 2:

Now behold, Boaz came from Bethlehem and said to the reapers, "May the LORD be with you." And they said to him, "May the LORD bless you." Then Boaz said to his servant who was in charge of the reapers, "Whose young woman is this?" And the servant in charge of the reapers answered and said, "She is the young Moabite woman who returned with Naomi from the land of Moab. And she said, 'Please let me glean and gather after the reapers among the sheaves.' Thus she came and has remained from the morning until now; she has been sitting in the house for a little while." (NASB)

A quick interruption is due here. Three quick context clues will make certain we get the picture:

#1—Regardless of where you live or in what time period, when it's harvest time the owner of the field will come make sure all is proceeding well. I saw this as a kid in western Oklahoma and Kansas and we see it in the story of Boaz. Regardless of how busy, the owner wants to be close for that critical moment in farming.

#2—In Boaz's day, there was no combine. The grain was harvested with hand sickles, stacked in sheaves, and then threshed using sledges and winnowing forks. It was an effective method but labor-intensive and a bit inefficient.

#3—Part of that inefficiency was accounted for in Moses' Law. The sickle method leaves quite a bit of fallen grain behind. Further, the circular cuts left corners of the rectangular fields un-harvested. But God commanded Israel to let the fallen pieces and corners alone so that those in need could provide for themselves. They were allowed to follow after the harvest workers and picking up all the leftovers.

With that in mind, turn back to the text and verses 8-16:.

Then Boaz said to Ruth, "Listen carefully, my daughter. Do not go to glean in another field; furthermore, do not go on from this one, but stay here with my maids. Let your eyes be on the field which they reap, and go after them. Indeed, I have commanded the servants not to touch you. When you are thirsty, go to the water jars and drink from what the servants draw." Then she fell on her face, bowing to the ground and said to him, "Why have I found favor in your sight that you should take notice of me, since I am a foreigner?" And Boaz answered and said to her, "All that you have done for your mother-in-law after the death of your husband has been fully reported to me, and how you left your father and your mother and the land of your birth, and came to a people that you did not previously know. May the LORD reward your work, and your wages be full from the LORD, the God of Israel, under whose wings you have come to seek refuge." Then she said, "I have found favor in your sight, my lord, for you have comforted me and indeed have spoken kindly to your maidservant, though I am not like one of your maidservants."

And at mealtime Boaz said to her, "Come here, that you may eat of the bread and dip your piece of bread in the vinegar." So she sat beside the reapers; and he served her roasted grain, and she ate and was satisfied and had some left. When she rose to glean, Boaz commanded his servants, saying, "Let her glean even among the sheaves, and do not insult her. And also you shall purposely pull out for her some grain from the bundles and leave it that she may glean, and do not rebuke her." (NASB)

It is a beautiful, moving story, is it not? Read the rest of it sometime. It's a great love story. You'll notice that throughout the tale, wise Ruth always hits on the key issue, as she does here. Ruth asks why she is being treated as an insider. She understands Boaz's great care for his own. That's grand, if somewhat expected. What she wonders is, "Why is this Moabite woman being treated like a member of the family?"

It's a great question. And Boaz gives a great answer that has depths we can't go into fully right now. We can note this: Boaz's answer makes it clear that he considers anybody seeking to serve the Lord to be part of his people. Their background doesn't matter. Their politics are unimportant. What matters is that anybody doing God's will, anyone trusting in Him, is worthy of the kinsman-redeemer's protection.

Jesus made this clear in His ministry as well. Remember His great statement about God's family in Matthew 12:47-50? Matthew records:

Someone said to Him, "Behold, Your mother and Your brothers are standing outside seeking to speak to You." But Jesus answered the one who was telling Him and said, "Who is My mother and who are My brothers?" And stretching out His hand toward His disciples, He said, "Behold My mother and My brothers! For whoever does the will of My Father who is in heaven, he is My brother and sister and mother." (NASB)

Jesus wasn't dismissing family obligations. He was emphasizing the important point displayed 1200 years earlier by Boaz. The kinsman-redeemer stands for his people, and his people include all those who do God's will.

This is why one can be far away, surrounded by people who look, sound, and smell nothing like the folks back in home, and yet if they are believers in Jesus one feels an immediate bond. You stand up for those people! In a very real way, they are your family. This is one of the most significant ways that Christianity changed the world.

The determination of Christians to stand up for disparate people is unique and astonishing. Believers in Jesus understand themselves as imitators of the great kinsman-redeemer. They further hear His commands that they care for all of the world, just as He does. Thus, despite their personal, sinful flesh and all the struggles of a selfish world, Christians routinely fight for those who are oppressed. It's been like that for 2000 years.

For example, our early Christian forefathers were shocked by the extremely low value the Romans and Greeks placed on human life. The Christians believed the Genesis statement that people are made in the image of God as the crowning glory of God's creation. As followers of Jesus, they said that human life was to be protected and honored regardless of its form or "quality." They actively opposed the depravity of the Greco-Roman society on such issues as infanticide, child abandonment, abortion, human sacrifices, gladiator contests, and suicide.

By the way, such behavior was not unique to the Greco-Roman cultures. Infanticide (especially of girls) was also common in India, China, and Japan. It took place in the Brazilian jungles, among the Inuit (Eskimos), in parts of pagan Africa, and among various Native Americans of both North and South America. In the Roman Empire, if unwanted babies were not directly killed, they were frequently abandoned. The Christians not only condemned child abandonment, they took these discarded children into their own homes.

Although severely persecuted, Christians never stopped promoting and sacrificing for the sanctity of human life. They felt it was their calling as kinsman-redeemers. Finally, in A.D. 374, Valentinian, a Christian emperor who was greatly influenced by Bishop Basil of Caesarea, outlawed infanticide and child abandonment. It was a major moment in the history of the world.

Professor Rodney Stark wrote a tremendous and interesting study of all this. In his book *How the West Won,* Dr. Stark shares:

> The early [churches'] opposition to abortion, along with their condemnation of infanticide and child abandonment, was a major factor in institutionalizing the sanctity of human life in the Western world ... . The sanctity of life, with the exception of abortion, is still largely present today."[45]

Values have consequences!

Our forefathers did the right thing and stood up for people in need because that's what our Lord did. Jesus stood up for His people. Look at the rest of our Garden of Gethsemane passage there in John 18:8-9:

> Jesus answered, "I told you that I am *He;* if therefore you seek Me, let these go their way," that the word might be fulfilled which He spoke, "Of those whom Thou hast given Me I lost not one." (NASB)

The kinsman-redeemer stands up for God's people. He does the right thing. It's what real grown-up men do. In 2007, a very intriguing movie was released titled *Lars and the Real Girl.* It's an artsy, thoughtful look at humanity that particularly delves into the question of what makes a man. One of the most brilliant exchanges in Nancy Oliver's script occurs between Lars [who struggles with mental illness] and his older brother:

> *Lars:* I was talking to Bianca, and she was saying that in her culture they have these rites of passage and rituals and

ceremonies. This whole kind of *thing* that you know when you do them or when you're done if you live through them that you know you're an adult. Doesn't that sound great?

Gus: It does.

Lars: How do you know?

Gus: How I know what?

Lars: That you are a man.

Gus: Nah, I couldn't tell you.

Lars: Okay, was it sex?

Gus: Um ... yeah, yeah ... It's a ... yeah yeah ... Well it's kind of sex ... (shaking head no) but it's not ... no ... it's not ... umm ...

I ... I don't know. I don't know. It's a good ... good question.

Lars: Yeah, but I have to know.

Gus: (In response to buzzer on dryer) Hold that thought. You know you should ask Dagmar (Gus' wife).

Lars: I did ask Dagmar. She said that I should ask you.

Gus: (folding laundry) You know I ... I can only give you my opinion.

Lars: That's all I want.

Gus: Well it's not like one thing or the other, okay? There's still a little kid inside, but you ... you grow up when you decide to do right, okay? And not what's right for you, what's right for everyone. Even when it hurts.

Lars: Like what?

Gus: Like ... you don't jerk people around, you know? And ... and you don't cheat on your woman. And you take care your family. You admit when you're wrong, or you try to any ways.

That's all I can think of, you know? It sounds like it's easy, and for some reason it's not.

Lars: I know. Because nothing is easy.

Gus: It's like [our] old man. He didn't have to take care of two kids alone. He could have given us to an orphanage or something. You know, people do that. But he loved us, and he tried to do right, even though he didn't know how and even though he had a broken heart.[46]

The growing-up problem isn't limited to Lars. The problem is with an entire culture. The film goes on to lament that far too few men are willing to grow up. In the words of Lars' brother, too few boys "do what's right" and thus choose to become men.

Are you a grown-up? Do your people know that you will stand up for them? Let me put it this way: Do they know that you would throw yourself on the grenade for them? That question takes us to the other great image in the Bible—a warrior.

THE BIBLICAL MAN IS A WARRIOR.

The warrior image is used so often in Scripture that we hardly recognize the original image of battle. Just consider these few passages built on the warrior concept:

- 2 Timothy 2:3 "Suffer hardship with me, as a good soldier of Christ Jesus." (NASB)

- Philemon 2 "...Archippus our fellow soldier, and to the church that meets in your home." (HCSB)

- Romans 13:12 "...let us lay aside the deeds of darkness and put on the armor of light." (NASB)

- James 5:8 "Take courage, for the coming of the Lord is near." (NLT)

- 1 Timothy 6:12 "Fight the good fight of faith" (NASB)

This is just a sampling; there are hundreds of other allusions and references throughout the Bible. The image God uses is clear: His man is a soldier. And the warrior puts his life on the line for others.

Read with me from 1 Samuel 14 and let's learn from the warrior Jonathan. Significant information on Jonathan's soldiering is found in verses 6, 12, and 13:

> Then Jonathan said to the young man who was carrying his armor, "Come and let us cross over to the garrison of these uncircumcised; perhaps the LORD will work for us, for the LORD is not restrained to save by many or by few." ... So the men of the garrison hailed Jonathan and his armor bearer and said, "Come up to us and we will tell you something." And Jonathan said to his armor bearer, "Come up after me, for the LORD has given them into the hands of Israel." Then Jonathan climbed up on his hands and feet, with his armor bearer behind him; and they fell before Jonathan, and his armor bearer put some to death after him. (NASB)

The piratical group known as the "sea-peoples" had finished a season of bouncing around the Mediterranean by settling on the coastal plain of Israel. Called Philistines in the Bible, these harsh pagans had become quite strong by Jonathan's day. They were using superior technology and fearsome warriors to pressure Israeli settlements and had become a serious threat to the young kingdom of Israel. Jonathan observed all this, of course, but he also noted something very important—the Philistines were overconfident. Seeing this, Jonathan took a calculated risk. He dashed forward and practiced an individualized form of shock-and-awe tactics. And what motivated Jonathan is important to understand. Jonathan's dad the king was back with the Israeli army, trapped and looking for a break in the Philistine noose that was closing about them. In fact, King Saul's army had begun dissipating in panic. Jonathan's attack gave his people the breakthrough they needed. He made a way for all his countrymen to pierce the Philistine line, and Israel's army followed-up this opportunity very effectively, breaking the siege.

Heroic acts like that are what real men do. They fight for right. Though such battles are actually rarely physical, the biblically-minded man fights for good according to that kind of warrior ethos. Whether the struggle is material or immaterial (emotional, relational, mental, spiritual), God empowers men to fight like Jonathan.

The warrior puts his life on the line because it is the right thing to do, not because people applaud him. Sometimes, people don't appreciate him at all. Still, he fights for right. Dr. David Grossman, a retired Army Ranger, comments on this in his book *On Killing:*

> One Vietnam veteran, an old retired colonel, once said this to me: "Most of the people in our society are sheep. They are kind, gentle, productive creatures who can only hurt one another by accident. Then there are the wolves," the old war veteran said, "and the wolves feed on the sheep without mercy."
>
> Do you believe there are wolves out there that will feed on the flock without mercy? You better believe it. There are evil men in this world and they are capable of evil deeds. You cannot forget that or pretend it is not so. There is no safety in denial.
>
> "Then there are sheepdogs," he went on, "and I'm a sheepdog. I live to protect the flock and confront the wolf." Let me expand on this old soldier's excellent model of the sheep, wolves, and sheepdogs. The sheep generally do not like the sheepdog. He looks a lot like the wolf. He has fangs and the capacity for violence. The difference, though, is that the sheepdog must not, cannot and will not ever harm the sheep. Any sheepdog who intentionally harms the lowliest little lamb will be punished and removed.
>
> Still, the sheepdog disturbs the sheep. He is a constant reminder that there are wolves in the land. They would prefer that he didn't tell them where to go, or give them traffic tickets, or stand at the ready in our airports in camouflage fatigues holding an M-16. The sheep would much

rather have the sheepdog cash in his fangs, spray paint himself white, and go, "Baa." Until the wolf shows up! Then the entire flock tries desperately to hide behind one lonely sheepdog.[47]

Now, the analogy is overstated and a little simplistic. Yet the point is accurate: the kinsman-redeemer is a sheepdog. He's a warrior who puts his life on the line. He does so even when people don't like him for it or are concerned for his safety. We see this in one of the great New Testament heroes, Epaphroditus. Ponder the Apostle Paul's description of Epaphroditus in Philippians 2:25-30:

> But I considered it necessary to send you Epaphroditus— my brother, coworker, and fellow soldier, as well as your messenger and minister to my need— since he has been longing for all of you and was distressed because you heard that he was sick. Indeed, he was so sick that he nearly died. However, God had mercy on him, and not only on him but also on me, so that I would not have one grief on top of another. For this reason, I am very eager to send him so that you may rejoice when you see him again and I may be less anxious. Therefore, welcome him in the Lord with all joy and hold men like him in honor, because he came close to death for the work of Christ, risking his life to make up what was lacking in your ministry to me. (HCSB)

Epaphroditus and Jonathan were warriors, one spiritual and one physical, and are held up as examples for us all. And we must note that their most noble and important battles weren't physical. Don't shallowly assume that the physical battles are most significant. It's exactly opposite, in fact! Jonathan's hard-fought friendship with David receives much more attention in the Bible than his wars. Paul's friends like Epaphroditus fought spiritual battles that mattered most. As Paul told them—and us—we battle not against flesh and blood, but against spiritual powers. Christian men and Christian women are to be warriors in the Spirit. If you think physical battle is tough, and it is, remember, that non-physical conflicts are much more severe.

Looking at this point in the Scriptures, Hailey Dalrymple of our pulpit team sent me this painful story:

> In 2008, a guy named Bruce Dickson auditioned for American Idol. When they interviewed him before his audition, the interviewer asked about the necklace he was wearing. It was a gold chain with a small key attached. He claimed that he was a Christian and a virgin. In an effort to honor his future wife, he wears the "key to her heart" around his neck to represent his purity. His father has an identical gold chain around his neck, only his necklace has a small locket attached. Bruce explained that when he does marry his future wife, his dad will give her the locket necklace. The media had a ball with this story. He was mocked and made fun of for several weeks afterwards. MTV called his story "Bizarre."[48]

Now, Bruce may have lacked a little wisdom in his sharing, but look at what these men are doing. They are fighting for purity and honor for Bruce's future wife! And in that stand they faced a firefight as fierce as anything going down in the back streets of Aleppo. But no matter the opposition, the sheepdog—the warrior—fights on.

THE WARRIOR FIGHTS FOR GOD, BY GOD'S DIRECTION.

We're going to look at a positive and a negative example of this. First, for the negative, we'll consider the Old Testament general Joab. We don't have space to cite all the passages about Joab, so let me summarize:

- Joab probably ranks in the top ten military tacticians of antiquity.

- He was a stirring organizer, a gifted strategist, and a talented leader.

- But make no mistake; Joab obeyed orders from King David only when he felt like it.

- Joab made it clear that he fought only for his own "honor" (a fancy term for personal pride).

For example, one time Joab disagreed with David about a matter of policy. David wanted to show leniency toward another great commander, Abner. Joab did not. Joab pretended that he was concerned for David's kingdom, when in reality Joab only wanted revenge on Abner. 2 Samuel 3:26-27 tells us what Joab did next:

> When Joab came out from David, he sent messengers after Abner, and they brought him back from the well of Sirah; but David did not know it. So when Abner returned to Hebron, Joab took him aside into the middle of the gate to speak with him privately and there he struck him in the belly so that he died. (NASB)

Joab fought for his own desires, not for God's will. While working on this chapter, I was writing with a friend about Joab. The next day my buddy sent me a great summary:

> I spent the evening reading all about Joab. What a tragic figure he was! As you observed in your notes, he was obviously a talented military leader, but also a slave to his own "honor." In the end, even David couldn't look past Joab's failings, and instructed Solomon to "not let his (Joab's) gray head go down to Sheol in peace." (1 Kings 2:6) Not exactly a glowing performance review from the boss after a career of service![49]

Friends, listen up. If you don't fight under the King's direction, it doesn't matter how strong a battler you are. Your performance review at the *bema* judgment seat of Jesus (Romans 14:10; 2 Corinthians 5:1) will yield pitifully small rewards unless you fight for God and do it God's way.

Now, let's examine a more positive example, the Apostle Paul. We are introduced to Paul's warrior ethic in 2 Timothy 2:3-5:

> Suffer hardship with me, as a good soldier of Christ Jesus. No soldier in active service entangles himself in the affairs of everyday life, so that he may please the one who enlisted him as a soldier. And also if anyone competes as an athlete,

he does not win the prize unless he competes according to
the rules. (NASB)

Who is Paul trying to please? Himself? No! There's none of that Joab
nonsense. He's fighting for God and by God's direction. There are clear
rules for the warrior. Fighting for the Lord and by His instruction is a
must for the one who wants to win.

In his *Idylls of the King*, Alfred, Lord Tennyson tells the great story
of Gareth and Lynette. Gareth is the youngest of three brothers, the
two older of which have already left home to serve King Arthur. Gareth
is dying to follow them, but his mother holds him home, trying to protect her boy who is no longer a boy. Mom begs Gareth to stay, be content to chase the deer in the woods near their home, and marry "some
comfortable bride." But his heart yearns to leave and live the life of a
man, and his answer shows it. Ruminate on this brilliance:

> Man am I grown, a man's work must I do.
> Follow the deer? Follow the Christ, the King,
> Live pure, speak true, right wrong, follow the King.
> Else, wherefore born?

The Apostle Paul is surely an inspiration for Gareth. Paul teaches us to
fight for the Lord and by His direction. Otherwise, why are we even
here? It just doesn't make sense for God to empower us, outfit us as
warriors, and we miss the whole battle. This reminds me of one last
story. Listen to Pastor Steve Lawson from his book *Men Who Win*:

> The year was 1968. It was my senior year in high school, and
> we had a pretty good football team. Despite the fact that I
> was the quarterback.

> We were undefeated and ready to play our arch rivals, who
> were also undefeated, in the biggest game of the year. The
> stage was set for a schoolboy showdown, certainly one of
> the most important events in our young lives.

> It was Friday afternoon. We went into our gym, a big domed
> coliseum, to get dressed. The routine was to put on out uni-
> forms and go into the coliseum and "get our game face on."

We'd lie flat on our backs and think about the game. We'd just stare at the ceiling and visualize executing the plays and how we were going to beat our opponent.

There were about sixty of us in the pitch dark gym. It was so still, you could hear a pin drop. Suddenly, it was time to go to the stadium. Our coach came in and softly said, "Alright, men, let's get on the bus and go to the game."

My heart was pounding! I grabbed my helmet and shoes. We tiptoed out in our stocking feet, got on the bus, and headed to the stadium. The scene was electric. The whole community had packed the stadium.

We blew our rivals out of the water! The score was 35-0 at halftime. We didn't even punt. Five possessions, five touchdowns. The final score was 41-6. What a blowout!

After the game, everyone was elated! The student body, the parents, the band, the faculty—everybody was excited! As we came off the field and loaded the bus for the jubilant ride home, our fans were cheering and pounding us on the head!

It seemed like everyone was at the gym when our bus pulled up. We got off and had to fight through the crowd again. Everybody was slapping us on the back, cheering. Everybody was singing the school fight song; the band was playing.

The locker room was complete bedlam. Everybody was boxing, jostling each other, and popping one another with towels.

I slipped into the coliseum to be alone and began peeling off my jersey and pads. I replayed the whole game in my mind, savoring every play. I was replaying the first play, the second play, and so on.

As I was peeling off my jersey, I looked across the coliseum and saw the figure of a body lying at midcourt. The red exit song—the only light in the gym—was shining over the silhouette of this motionless body.

I had thought I was the only person in that pitch dark coliseum. I walked over and looked down at the figure and saw that it was a person. He had his full football uniform on—number 29. I didn't know if he was dead or alive.

I nudged him with my foot, gently. As soon as I did, BOOM! He shot up, put his helmet on, and said, "Let's get on the bus and go to the game!"

I said, "The game's over." (The funny thing is, we didn't even miss ol' number 29.)

I said, "It was the biggest game of our lives! We won, 41-6! You missed the whole thing." My friend had apparently stayed up late the night before and when he laid down, he went to sleep. For good.

Men, wake up and get in the game. Don't miss out on the greatest opportunity of your life; to win the race that God has set before you. Don't buy into the world's seductive message of position, prestige, and possessions. Don't go to sleep on the broad path that leads to destruction. Stay on the narrow path that leads to life. Get out of the rat race … and into the right race.[50]

The idea of standing for right seems laughable today. A culture awash with relativism questions whether "right" is even knowable. Grown males, trained to be selfish children in thought, look to their own pleasure and never consider standing up to evil. The few visible warriors for good tend to be female—a laudable fact made lamentable by the absence of male voices—and men have remained boys. The solution is a return to the great images of manhood given to us in Scripture: the kinsman-redeemer and warrior. May we live those images out in our own lives and spread their influence all around us.

CHAPTER 5

A REAL MAN THINKS AND LEARNS

CHAPTER SUMMARY: Men are rather often treated like children of the ninetenth century—expected to be seen and not heard. Because of this and the natural human tendencies toward pride and laziness, men today find it convenient to be slothful in their continuous development. God frowns on this and calls men instead to investigate and understand His world and His word. In effect, God commands His men to grow up and keep on growing.

LIFE CHANGE OBJECTIVE: That we are lifetime learners.

A MAN IS AN IDIOT.

Sometime during the twentieth century, the following developed as a stock characterization of men: A man is an idiot who has little discipline, especially between the ears. A man is expected to be nothing but an eternally adolescent male who is hopelessly incapable of real, sustained, updated thought. The world is always passing him by. Just watch television, especially the sit-coms and commercials, for the *zeitgeist* to pound your sensibilities. Nearly every male is depicted as an oaf. (It is also worth noting that many men have foolishly and selfishly bought into and furthered this image.)

We all see such depictions frequently. But here's what is really fascinating: society as a whole now regrets the consequences. There is widespread consternation over the results of men being trained to be thoughtless idiots.

My mail was quite interesting when I preached these lessons on biblical manhood. People that normally agree with me on very little were suddenly yelling "Hear, hear!" As we discussed the lamentable state of manhood in the western world, I received a great volume of positive mail. I even received a note from an atheist applauding the need to return manhood to a healthy base.

Why is everybody jumping on board with this cry for men to be real men and not empty-headed dummies? Because everybody with eyes now understands that you cannot build a sustainable society with a bunch of empty dummies. C. S. Lewis' warning rings very true:

> We make men without chests and expect of them virtue and enterprise. We laugh at honour and are shocked to find traitors in our midst. We castrate and bid the geldings be fruitful.[51]

Our culture has worked very hard to castrate men, especially regarding their intellect. But in contrast to our men-are-really-stupid nonsense stands God's true calling. God expects real men to develop and grow their minds. God made men to learn and think and keep learning and growing for a lifetime. It's how people fulfill our calling to glorify God. Because we are made in the image of the intelligent God—and not merely evolved stupidity—we pursue a lifetime of learning.

The world is waking up to the fact that the twentieth-century model of the idiot man is a dangerous dead-end. One of the most influential magazines in the world, *The Economist*, sported a cover recently that asked, "Will we ever invent anything this useful again?"[52] Tellingly, the picture parodied the male thinker by the sculptor Rodin, seated on a toilet. The idea was that men who think help change the world. Men who are taught to be dumb do not.

Of course this applies to everyone, males and females, young and old. God expects each person to develop intellectually. But for the most part it is modern men who have the opposite message pounded into their brains. Males today are told that you are dumb and the world wants it that way. For males over 15 years of age the current cultural mantra is: If you're going to be liked as a real man, you better remain an old-school idiot.

REAL MEN WORK TO UNDERSTAND AND SHAPE GOD'S WORLD.

Friends, I propose we leave that failed lunacy behind. Instead, let's turn to God's Word to learn about real manhood. Real men work to understand and shape God's world. Specifically, they think through situations and discern what needs to be done. There's a great summary of this in 1 Chronicles 12:32:

> From the tribe of Issachar, there were 200 leaders of the tribe with their relatives. All these men understood the temper of the times and knew the best course for Israel to take. (NLT)

REAL MEN THINK THROUGH SITUATIONS AND DISCERN WHAT NEEDS TO BE DONE (1 CHRONICLES 12:32).

1 Chronicles 12 is describing the nature of the warriors who joined David at Hebron. And the text is trying to answer a really important question. The author is thinking through how David and his men changed the world. You see, before David there was no such thing as a truly unified Israel making an impact on the world stage. The Israelites had lived in Canaan 400 years and never fully taken possession of the land. But after David, Israel is a force with which to be reckoned.

The Chronicler is considering what helped David get over that tipping point. Obviously, warriors played a big role. That's why they are listed in this text in the next verse (vs. 33).

> From the tribe of Zebulun, there were 50,000 skilled warriors. They were fully armed and prepared for battle and completely loyal to David. (NLT)

But those warriors aren't enough. Look again at the companion thought in verse 32. The warriors don't win without people who can think through what needs to be done. This explains why the subject is so seriously important to the world today. Even if men become the warriors they are meant to be, it does no good unless they can also *think!* Do you want to change the world? Do you want a tipping point in your country? Then you better train men to think things through and act accordingly.

Speaking of thinking things through, let's take a moment and think about thinking. Not long ago, I said to a crowd of about 1000 persons, "Raise your hand if it seems to you that our society is too rushed to think effectively." About 950 hands went up. I continued, "Now, keep your hand up if you think that statement also applies to you individually. Keep your hand up if you are often too rushed to think effectively." Very few of the 950 lowered their arms, and some of the other hands which had been in laps were raised.

God's person is intended to understand the world. He does this by developing comprehension; by thinking. Yet we live in a world where thinking things through is incredibly rare. Randall Satchell of my pulpit team at our church wrote me the following note as we discussed this:

> No one seems to have enough time in the day to do all that needs to be done. We all know we need to slow down, to bring some sanity back into our schedules. Anyone who has worked on business problems, engineering problems, or even homework problems has experienced the joy of discarding a quick solution for a better one. This will usually occur after one spends time deeply considering the pros, cons, and alternatives.
>
> Now contemplate the opposite of this phenomenon: making decision after decision without taking the time to think through any of them. What strikes me is that when we rush to work, rush from meeting to meeting with little or no downtime in between, work late, rush home, and then repeat six or more days every week, there are likely hundreds of decisions we make each month which are not the best decisions. They may not even be good decisions![53]

Randall is correct. Let's read from the most popular song ever written, Psalm 23:

A Psalm of David.
The LORD is my shepherd, I shall not want.
He makes me lie down in green pastures;
He leads me beside quiet waters. (NASB)

What kind of waters? Quiet. The King James Version reads "still waters." When a person follows God's lead, part of his or her norm is stillness. Quiet. If one wants to think, a certain amount of peace and quiet is needed. In order to fulfill God's calling to love Him with all of our minds, we must build stillness into our daily, weekly, and annual rhythms. Yet, I am often told some variation of this statement, "Pastor Wayne, I just don't have time to fight through all the distractions beating down on me!"

I understand. However, if you tell me that you simply cannot find space to think, that you cannot locate peace and quiet in your hurried life, then I can say with near-certainty that you are not letting the Lord lead you as Shepherd. If there is no regular quiet water beside which you can contemplate, then you are not following the Good Shepherd. And it won't be long before you are diminishing in usefulness as an under-shepherd in His world.

I rather like Thoreau's solution. Look what he wrote in *Walden*: "I had three chairs in my house—one for solitude, two for friendship, three for society."[54] There is much goofiness that passes for thought in that book, but that wise statement implies a beneficial balance. Healthy thought does not require becoming a hermit. There is great thinking that only comes through one-on-one and group interactions. Thus all three chairs are important. But in our day, Thoreau's second and third chairs are almost always filled, especially through our continually-connected devices. Because the crowd is always with us, we lose the solitude and silence of the first chair altogether.

There's another, related problem that keeps us from thinking things through. We don't like to think about how we think. That's partly why we stay so hurried, so we won't have to stop and look in the intellectual mirror. Have you ever wondered why really bad ideas

get such a strong hold on society? Have you ever considered why supposedly smart people keep spewing forth idiotic solutions generation
after generation?

As one among thousands of examples, consider this one. A hundred years ago, a strong consensus of scientists agreed that drinking
water laced with radiation would promote good health. Journalist
Theodore Gray summarizes the phenomenon:

> A century ago radioactivity was new, exciting and good for
> you—[there were] radium pendants for rheumatism, all-
> natural radon water for vigor, uranium blankets for arthritis
> and thorium-laced medicine for digestion (you don't even
> want to know about the radioactive suppositories).[55]

Seriously! Radon was popular with the elites and the press because a
consensus of scientists proclaimed it fact. But the results were tragic,
leading to eventual headlines like the 1932 *Wall Street Journal* headline
"The Radium Water Worked Fine, Until His Jaw Came Off." Many
wealthy people died of radiation poisoning. They died because they
didn't consider the method and thinking behind the research.

God has a solution for this kind of radioactive danger. Turn one
book to the east in your Bible, to Proverbs 14:8:

> The wisdom of the prudent is to understand his way (NASB)

The HCSB translation reads, "The sensible man's wisdom is to
consider his way." See the point? Think about the operating system.
Think about your ways, your means of making decisions. Ponder on
how you acquire information and determine truth. The fancy word for
that is epistemology. Proverbs says to consider epistemology—how you
know that you know what you know.

Are magazines or Facebook articles your source of decision-mak-
ing wisdom? Do you just do whatever some authority figure tells you?
Do you take your marching orders from some political party or from
political correctness? Slide down to verse 15:

> The naive believes everything,
> But the prudent man considers his steps. (NASB)

This is why silly ideas get a hold on the masses. Never underestimate the power of a bad idea on a large crowd! Bad ideas sometimes sound smart; but they can't hold up to real reason. There is a serious flaw in the thinking, but people don't want to work it out. Humans often won't do the heavy lifting required to think about the flaws in human reasoning. That's why people don't think things through. It's why so few can discern what really needs to be done.

By contrast, you and I are going to be a part of a great change. We are going to lead a charge of real thought. God wants to develop women and men who think things through and thus know how to make a difference socially. Values have consequences!

REAL MEN KNOW HOW TO MAKE A DIFFERENCE SOCIALLY (MICAH 6:8).

Look at these powerful summary verses from Micah 6:8 and Isaiah 1:17:

> He has told you, O man, what is good;
> And what does the LORD require of you
> But to do justice, to love kindness,
> And to walk humbly with your God? (NASB)

> Learn to do good; Seek justice,
> Reprove the ruthless;
> Defend the orphan,
> Plead for the widow. (NASB)

The context in each prophet's argument is the same. God is telling people how to live their grace relationship with God out in society. These simple steps are how God's people make a difference in the world. This is the key to a healthy social life: do justice; love mercy; walk humbly; fight to protect the weak.

That's pretty straightforward, right? Except, we have a big problem. In our day, females are seen as champions of these things. That's good, except, often, *only* females are considered capable of handling social issues. There's an assumption that men have no clue how to make a real difference in people's lives.

After I taught on this, a lady sent me the following pop culture example:

> Wayne, on a recent episode of *Modern Family*, (Dad) Phil and (Mom) Claire's children [Haley, Alex, and Luke] are dealing with issues concerning their friends and social lives. All three children come barging into the living room looking for their mom so she can solve their problems. They all begin panicking because they can't find her—all the while, Phil is standing right there, wanting them to come to him. He finally forces them to sit down and share their struggles. Later that day, when he tries to fix their problems on his own, it all goes wrong and blows up in his face. All of Phil's children are angry with him and he is left looking like an idiot—a prime example of what you are discussing in the manhood series.[56]

This illustration from television is nothing new. Take any episode of *I Love Lucy, The Flintstones,* or *The Jetsons* and you see the same story. Dudes, let's be honest. Guys have brought a lot of this on themselves. Because men haven't lived out Isaiah 1 and Micah 6, the world has somewhat understandably reached the conclusion that modern men never will make a social difference. Are you content with that? Are you willing to remain where manhood is today? Or, do you want to make a difference in the world?

If you desire to live out the calling given by Micah and Isaiah, then do what your Christian forefathers did! Be like William Wilberforce when he stood up against injustices such as slavery. Love mercy like Richard Wurmbrand. "Prisoner Number One" to the communist Romanian authorities, Pastor Wurmbrand was horribly tortured from 1948-1956. Yet he responded with mercy toward his captors and love for all. After his release, instead of demanding revenge, he said, "God will judge us not according to how much we endured, but how much we could love. I am a witness for the Christians in communist prisons that they could love. They could love God and men."[57] Men have made massive social contributions in the past, and they must do so once again.

REAL MEN KNOW THAT THIS WORLD ISN'T THE END OR ALL THERE IS IN LIFE (ECCLESIASTES 12:13-14).

Of course, wise men who understand the world also realize that this world isn't the end. Listen to Solomon's thoughtful conclusion in Ecclesiastes 12:

> The conclusion, when all has been heard, is: fear God and keep His commandments, because this applies to every person. For God will bring every act to judgment, everything which is hidden, whether it is good or evil. (NASB)

The New Testament goes on to tell us where this revelation occurs: at the judgment seat of Christ for Christians and at the Great White Throne judgment for those who reject Jesus. Revelation 20 describes the judgment of all who reject Christ, a reckoning of great power and pain. 1 Corinthians 3 and 2 Corinthians 5 detail the judgment seat of Christ for believers, describing the administration of rewards for eternity. Thus, everything in this life will be judged before the eternal days come. Therefore, real men look ahead. They order their days not just for here and now, but, for then and there.

Wise people live in light of eternity. They overcome the short-sightedness that has plagued every generation. Those who work best in God's world now are those who are cognizant of the world to come. That's what made Wilberforce bold and Wurmbrand merciful. Their papers and letters are full of references to judgment and to heaven. It's what made Billy Graham consistently the most trusted and popular person on the planet. He gained this world by focusing his attention on the next. And that's the kind of person God wants you to be. To get there, you have to consistently discern these days and hold them up for examination in light of the ones to come.

REAL MEN WORK TO UNDERSTAND GOD'S WORD.

I'm convinced the decline in manhood began in the twentieth century because it was the first century in which men were not leading in the perusal of Scripture. In the famous 1959 painting by Norman Rockwell entitled *Sunday Morning*, there is a stunning and accurate visual representation of this decline. It shows a mother, two daughters, and a son walking across the living room, dressed and with Bibles, and headed to church.

And what is Dad doing? He's staying home and reading the paper in his pajamas, slippers, and robe. He is slouched down in the chair so as not to be seen by them. Dad is rightly trying to grasp what's going on in the world; however, he's missing the critically important filter of knowing how it all relates to God's Word.

The boy is looking at Dad and leaning towards his father's chair. He is taking his cues from Dad and moving away from those who are going to study the Bible. Rockwell—who is never given enough credit for his depth of thought—captures a massive change that he was feeling in the country and especially in his beloved New England.

In U.S. history, there have been many seasons when church attendance was low. For example, before Jonathan Edwards and the Great Awakening, church attendance was far lower than it is today. There had always been people who rejected Jesus as depicted in the Bible; always Americans who rejected the Savior who is the only way to heaven.

But those past skeptical deists and atheists knew it was important to study and know the Scriptures. Even those who spurned Christ saw the Bible as foundational to western civilization. And even when church attendance was low, it was incredibly rare for a family to go to church without Dad. Men were always leading their homes in the Bible.

But the post-WWII world endured a sea change. Norman Rockwell felt the change, which has fully flowered in our time. Men have stopped leading through God's Word, and manhood has declined in direct relation to the decline in biblical literacy.

By contrast, real men know the primacy of God's words. Psalm 119:162 captures the idea:

> I rejoice at Your word
> As one who finds great treasure. (NKJV)

Real men work to understand the treasure of God's Word, and that gets passed on to the next generation. Boys and girls are looking to you guys.

The kids without dads are looking to you men. And by God's amazing grace, men—even dorky dudes like us—can have an awesome impact. When we discuss the Bible naturally; when we are spotted reading the Bible; when we engage with God's people around His Word; it creates a legacy of power for the next generation.

REAL MEN GROW UP BOLDLY DESPITE (AND THROUGH) LIFE'S STRUGGLES.

Real men work to understand God's Word. They work to understand and shape God's world. And real men grow up boldly despite all the struggles of life this side of heaven. Look at the opening verses (1-7) of the letter from Paul to Timothy in 2 Timothy 1:

> Paul, an apostle of Christ Jesus by God's will, for the promise of life in Christ Jesus: To Timothy, my dearly loved son. Grace, mercy, and peace from God the Father and Christ Jesus our Lord. I thank God, whom I serve with a clear conscience as my ancestors did, when I constantly remember you in my prayers night and day. Remembering your tears, I long to see you so that I may be filled with joy, clearly recalling your sincere faith that first lived in your grandmother Lois, then in your mother Eunice, and that I am convinced is in you also. Therefore, I remind you to keep ablaze the gift of God that is in you through the laying on of my hands. For God has not given us a spirit of fearfulness, but one of power, love, and sound judgment. (HCSB)

REAL MEN FIND COURAGE IN GOD'S PLAN (2 TIMOTHY 1:1-7).

Paul is writing to his protégé, and he reminds Timothy that real men find courage in God's plan. Paul has known this young man a long time, and Paul knows that Pastor Timothy is facing hardship and opposition in his life and his work. So he reminds Timothy that God's hand has always been on his life. Timothy's mother and grandmother were godly women who trusted Jesus and followed Him. It seems likely that Timothy's Dad was not in the picture.

Yet, it doesn't matter what is one's physical background, because every Christian's spiritual heritage is incredibly rich! Paul discussed this in the first chapter of his letter to the Ephesian church (1:3-5), the same one Timothy pastored for years:

> Blessed be the God and Father of our Lord Jesus Christ, who has blessed us with every spiritual blessing in the heavenly places in Christ, just as He chose us in Him before the foundation of the world, that we should be holy and blameless before Him. In love He predestined us to adoption as sons through Jesus Christ to Himself, according to the kind intention of His will. (NASB)

Men and women, I know you get defeated. Maybe the economy stinks, or you are very worried about your kids, or you are struggling through life battles and feel all alone. I know because the Bible says life is that way. I know because I feel the same things. But we cannot quit moving forward. Look at that truth we just read. Draw strength from what you know is true. Draw strength from God's plan and keep on. As Paul said to Timothy, kindle afresh the gift of God. Grow up boldly! Don't be timid! Show power, love, sound judgment, and discipline.

Let me introduce you to two men from my own experience: we'll call these two guys Saul and Paul. Saul's wife committed adultery and fled with the other guy, leaving Saul with a young son abandoned by the mother. Saul became immobilized with grief—an understandable reaction. But, Saul refused to function at all. When we would try to lovingly discuss power and love and sound judgment, Saul's only answer was despair.

Eventually that despair was directed at God. "How could a loving God do this to me?" Saul would cry out. We encouraged Saul to keep talking to God about those questions, to wrestle hard with the Lord. We read Habakkuk together, and David and Job—all people who faced similar despair and wrestled with God about it. But Saul didn't want to really engage with God. He just wanted to complain. He refused to keep learning and growing.

In fact, Saul soon tired of talking with us. He cut off all his Christian buddies and turned to alcohol for solace. He quit coming to church. Saul started sleeping with women out of marriage. He began to rant on a blog all day, trading deep thought for shallow tripe. And eventually his son became just like him. I saw the son not too long ago. He reeked of dope and refused to look me in the eye. It was heartbreaking.

Now, about the same time Saul was going through hell, Paul's life took a similar horrible twist. Paul's wife also ran off, though she abandoned her covenant for another woman. She left Paul all alone with a little boy and a shattered heart. As we sat and grieved with Paul, he went through the same emotions as Saul had. He was also angry and scared; and all that eventually became directed at God.

But where Saul sneered and refused to listen, Paul really engaged. He yelled and cried. Then he looked and listened to God's answers in Scripture. And Paul became deeply impressed with Jeremiah's truth—the same truth found in Habakkuk and Job and others. Paul became enamored with the truth that God's plan is awesome, even through the pain he endured.

Paul became a man of courage because he rested in the Lord's plan. He kindled afresh the gifts and calling of being a follower of Jesus. My friend Paul, like Timothy in our text, had a powerful positive impact on his son and those around him. Paul became a bold man—as refreshingly bold as Saul was bitter.

That's the choice this Timothy text above is offering you. Life will suck. Jesus promised that this side of heaven we will deal with evil. You can either become a bold one who fights the good fight to rekindle His trust in Christ or you can slink into timid bitterness.

I am not a beer lover, but guys tell me that they love a bold beer that's not bitter. When I worked in Germany, beer was a major topic of discussion, and the consensus among my friends was that Braunschweiger Mumme was the real deal: a very bold Schwarzbier that was never bitter. Similarly, to the Lord who loves your soul this is a huge topic. Be bold, never bitter. Find courage in God's plan.

REAL MEN LEARN FROM THEIR MISTAKES (2 TIMOTHY 4:11).

Now, if they are going to grow despite life's struggles, real men also must learn from their mistakes. The pains through which we learn and grow aren't only external. We must learn from our own goofs as well. Let's read 2 Timothy 4:11:

> Only Luke is with me. Pick up Mark and bring him with you, for he is useful to me for service. (NASB)

As one who has made many mistakes and sinned far too often, I find this one of the most encouraging verses in the Bible. You see, the Mark mentioned here is John Mark. He was a wealthy and possibly spoiled Roman citizen who was also a Jew. He became an early follower of Jesus and was member of one of the most influential families in early Christianity.

Mark went on a mission trip with the Apostle Paul, only to flame out part way through. In the face of blisteringly fierce opposition, Mark turned tail and went home to Mommy. The fallout didn't end there. John Mark's cousin Barnabas was Paul's partner in missions, and the partners ended up splitting over the John Mark fiasco.

Yet look at what Paul says these many years later, "Mark is useful." That gives me chills. John Mark learned from his mistake. He repented of his cowardly sin (and that's what cowardice always is—it is sin). Instead of continuing to turn tail and run, Mark turned to and trusted the Lord. In fact, he was so effectively reengineered that God used Mark to record one of the most important books ever written: *The Gospel of Jesus according to Mark*.

This is what real men do. We don't hide our mistakes. We own them and use them as levers for rising up and seeing God use us more fully. We get scared, but we turn to the Lord. Paul understood this quite well. Consider what he wrote in his first letter to Timothy (1:15-16):

> It is a trustworthy statement, deserving full acceptance, that Christ Jesus came into the world to save sinners, among whom I am foremost of all. And yet for this reason I found mercy, in order that in me as the foremost, Jesus Christ might demonstrate His perfect patience, as an example for those who would believe in Him for eternal life. (NASB)

Paul knows himself. He knows his weaknesses. And he knows that the most important lesson he can learn from his mistakes is how to rely on

God's grace. How do you learn from your mistakes and press on? You do so by resting in the hand of your Father who is developing you for your ultimate blessing, for others' benefit, and for God's glory.

REAL MEN REMEMBER THEIR CALLING (1 TIMOTHY 1:5, 18).

If one is going to successfully keep pressing on through all the muck of this life—if one is going to keep growing in God's Word and learning and thinking and studying God's world—then one must remember the bottom line of why we are here. Look at how God states it in verses 5 and 18 of 1 Timothy 1:

> But the goal of our instruction is love from a pure heart and a good conscience and a sincere faith.

> This command I entrust to you, Timothy, my son, in accordance with the prophecies previously made concerning you, that by them you may fight the good fight. (NASB)

God says to Timothy, me, and you: "Here's the bottom line, son. You are not here to have a good time. I hope you do, because I am gracious and give good things to enjoy. But your purpose is love. Love based on a good conscience (an ability to discern and think), a pure heart, and a sincere trust in the Lord."

You have to fight for this. You must work hard to remember your real calling. The world will try to distract you. Even good intentions will draw you off-base. But you must stand firm as a man who knows who he is and what he's here to do.

Years ago, my precious sweetheart was unhappy about something. I don't remember what, and neither does she. But we do remember the discussion that followed. I was trying desperately to make her happy. In that fascinating mix of motives and emotions involved in deepest friendship, I was laboring to make her happy. Frustrated with my efforts, she finally looked at me, scooted a Bible across the table and said: "Would you please show me where in here it says that your life's purpose is to make me happy?"

I was stunned. I started to reach for the Bible but knew enough Scripture to know that was hopeless. Janna went on: "Last time I checked, your purpose was to serve God with your all. You get off of that for anything—even my happiness—and we're doomed. You'll lose both your purpose *and* any hope of our happiness."

How do you fight through all the struggles? How do you keep on as a lifetime learner? You remember your purpose. Remember how Jesus put it? "Seek first God's kingdom and all these other things are added to you" (Matthew 6:33). I can testify that it works. I have a very happy wife, who finds joy in a partner who stays focused on my true calling to follow Jesus.

CHAPTER 6

A REAL MAN MAKES REAL FRIENDS

CHAPTER SUMMARY: God intends men to bond with and be genuine, loyal friends. The Lord gives instruction about relating rightly to peers, mentors, protégés and spouses.

LIFE CHANGE OBJECTIVE: That we make and are real friends.

In my college biology courses I was taught that male elephants, known as bulls, live solitary lives. They only come together for rare defense purposes. However, careful field research has shown that idea is far from accurate. Stanford's Caitlin O'Connell-Rodwell gives a great summary of what we've learned recently. In *Smithsonian*, she writes:

> Male elephants have a reputation as loners. But in Amboseli National Park in Kenya, where the longest-running studies on male elephants have been conducted, bulls have been observed to have a best friend with whom they associate for years. Another study, in Botswana, found that younger males seek out older males and learn social behaviors from them. In my studies [in Namibia's Etosha National Park] I'd noticed that males have not just one close buddy but several,

and that these large groups of males of mixed ages persisted for many years.[58]

Men, it seems that we could learn a great deal from elephants. You see, human bulls also need real friends. But in general the western male has been raised under the old idea of the elephant—solitary and meant to stay that way. Thus, males today have a very hard time making friends. In some ways, the situation is getting worse every year, especially for young men.

For generations, boys made friends by competing with each other. It's fact. Literature is rife with examples of men who make close buddies by fighting on the playground. Read Caesar or Livy or Sun Tzu; study Sam Houston or Andrew Jackson; watch an old John Wayne movie and you'll see what I'm describing. Men often become friends by competing, and sometimes, by even fighting with one another.

I personally experienced this. I started a ten-year close friendship with John Mutz by getting into a fight on the first grade playground. In second grade Eddie Rodriguez and Kevin Mikawa became by close buds of mine via the same method. In each case Mr. Coley—our old principal who had captained a destroyer during the Second World War—old Mr. Coley stood watch over the fight. He was there to make sure no permanent damage was done, that no one interfered, and that no one fought unfairly.

Compare that with our playgrounds today. Can you imagine the news crews hovering to shriek the exposé of the elementary principal who let the boys fight it out as boys? Of course, bullying is indeed evil! Bullying must not be tolerated. Mr. Coley, by the way, was very good at stopping bullies. They went in his office as wolves and came out toothless. We didn't know what he did in there, but it was the stuff of legend. No bully stood a chance with Captain Coley.

But our current over-reactive culture leaves no room for young men to compete or even fight with each other without calling in the FBI. And by the way, our elimination of all fighting has only made the pickings easier for the bullies. It's fascinating that scientists who would never dream of stopping bull elephants from fighting (which, by the way, is how they also become friends); who preach non-interference with elephants, would be horrified over two young boys wrestling. Guys today feel like they are Martians permanently bound on Venus, where everything is slanted against their nature. And thus, for every generation that goes by, men report having fewer and fewer close friends.

Yet men need real friends. And God's Word tells us about not only our need for friends, but also how to best meet that need. The Bible shows us how to make and keep real friends regardless of what planet we're stuck on. Ladies, these texts apply to you as well. I feel confident they will change your hearts also. However, I am going to direct my remarks to the dudes who are in desperate need of God's words on friendship.

MALE FRIENDSHIPS ARE CRITICALLY IMPORTANT.

We can summarize God's Word on this topic in a simple statement: male friendships are critically important. In 1 Samuel 18:1-4 we find a beautiful illustration of this truth:

> Now it came about when he [David] had finished speaking to Saul, that the soul of Jonathan [Saul's son] was knit to the soul of David, and Jonathan loved him as himself. And Saul took him that day and did not let him return to his father's house. Then Jonathan made a covenant with David because he loved him as himself. And Jonathan stripped himself of the robe that was on him and gave it to David, with his armor, including his sword and his bow and his belt. (NASB)

Of all the things God could have had written about David, the Lord spends a great deal of ink telling us about David's friendship with Jonathan. Space in the Scriptures is limited. Why use so much print on this covenant? It is because same-sex friends empower us.

SAME-SEX FRIENDS EMPOWER US (1 SAMUEL 18:1-4).

When you read the entire David-Jonathan saga, it becomes clear that neither man could have navigated life nearly so well without the other. David and Jonathan were like two climbers under extreme conditions. They roped themselves together for mutual protection, encouragement, and safety. That's what smart guys do for their friends. We rope together out of love for the friend and because we see our own need.

As a young adult, I contracted viral meningitis. It was my worst headache ever! My fever spiked over 106°; I was comatose for a short time; I could easily have died. It is a miracle that I came through the ordeal unscathed. And at least one of the tools God used to get me through that battle was a man named Mike.

Mike and I had met that summer as fellow employees of Pine Cove Camps. We thought a lot alike and became friends. And when I was in the hospital, Mike was only person who sat by my bedside every hour. He stayed there, praying for me, hour after hour in a hard chair. When my parents finally arrived from their long drive across two states, Mike met them and gave them the update.

Of course I thanked Mike. If you've been seriously ill, you know what an uplifting thing it is to know someone is with you, sitting with you, praying for you. I later asked Mike why he stayed with me through all that. And he quoted verse 3, "Then Jonathan made a covenant with David because he loved him as himself."

We also made a covenant. I stood as his best man in his wedding. He did the same at mine. We were there for the birth of each child and we drive the distance to catch up every year. I am empowered even today, knowing that if one of you called Michael and said, "Come right now, Wayne needs you." Mike would be here as fast as humanly possible, no questions asked.

Gentlemen, what about you? Have you let yourself bond with other men so that you are empowered, knowing someone has strong hold on the other end of your rope? Let me put it this way: Who will carry your casket? It takes six to pull that off, unless you weigh even less than I do. You need friends who lift you up—and not just in death. You need men who can empower you in life.

A couple hundred years after Jonathan and David, the Greek poet Homer picked up on the same idea. There is a great scene in Book X of Homer's *Iliad* where the Trojans have backed up the Greeks almost to their ships. The Greek generals have an emergency meeting where they ask for a volunteer to sneak behind enemy lines to possibly learn of the Trojan plans. A warrior named Diomedes volunteers, something in keeping with his greatness. Diomedes is that rarity in Greek literature—a truly noble person. But, before he heads out on the spy mission Diomedes makes the case for bringing a second man with him. Homer records Diomedes' wisdom:

> But let some other chosen warrior join,
> To raise my hopes, and second my design.
> By mutual confidence and mutual aid,
> Great deeds are done, and great discoveries made;
> The wise new prudence from the wise acquire,
> And one brave hero fans another's fire.[59]

A friend of mine once wrote a great commentary on this verse. He said:

> In six short lines Diomedes hits on as many benefits of having real friendships: raise hope, confirm plans, add confidence, help each other, increase wisdom, and fan bravery into fire.[60]

These benefits of real friendship can accrue to real men today just as surely as they did to those on the battlefields of ancient Greece, as soon as we are willing to "let some other chosen warrior join." Although I don't have space to look at it in detail, we should note that the same theme is also developed extensively in Shakespeare's writings. One of his major and repeated themes examines the ways real men empower other men.

HOMOSEXUAL BEHAVIOR IS NOT REAL FRIENDSHIP.

Speaking of Shakespeare, he also deals quite effectively with our second point: Homosexual behavior is not real friendship. It has become fashionable to see Shakespeare's strong male friendships as homo-erotic. Romeo and Mercutio, the guys in *Loves Labor Lost*, and many other men in Shakespeare's plays exhibit truly remarkable bonds with each other. The current *zeitgeist* sees this as homosexual, but such is not the case!

Tony Nuttall is the world's foremost authority on the bard and one of the greatest Shakespeare scholars of all time. Dr. Nuttall taught

Shakespeare for thirty years at Oxford and in a wonderful book that I highly recommend, he concludes: "It is difficult in the present age to play the part [of the male friends] without suggesting homosexual feeling in the background. I believe that this is a mistake."[61]

Nuttall goes on to show how homosexuality doesn't fit at all with Shakespeare's ethos or argument in most of the stories. Such a warped interpretation comes from the reader, not the author. The same holds true of those who try to say that Jonathan and David were homosexually committed. It's absurd and uneducated. Men can and do love each other as themselves, and it need not include sinful sexuality.

This brings up another reason male friendships are lagging. There is heightened concern today that the world will reach the wrong conclusion about guys who are close. Such is the core problem with the Boy Scouts of America opening their dens to practitioners of homosexuality. It erodes the biblical ideal of Jonathan and David by introducing a new and unwelcome dynamic.

I do not recommend the old TV show "Psych" as a moral compass. But I will say this for Steve Franks and the other writers of that show: they have read some Bible and some Shakespeare. They do an excellent job showing how two guys, Shawn and Gus, can be extremely close in friendship and it not be the least bit homosexual. (As characters, their unscriptural sexuality runs strongly the other direction.)

Remember the big idea: it is critically important for males to bond together with other dudes. That's why Russell Adams' article became so popular. In case you missed it, let me fill you in. In 2013, Russell Adams of the *Wall Street Journal* wrote a fun fluff piece—just a lighthearted, below-the-fold story. But embedded in that story was faithful, long-term friendship, and that masculine friendship factor caused the tale to go viral all over the globe. Here's a sample:

> Earlier this month, Brian Dennehy started a new job as chief marketing officer of Nordstrom Inc. In his first week, he pulled aside a colleague to ask a question: How hard it is for a nonemployee to enter the building? Mr. Dennehy doesn't have a particular interest in corporate security. He just doesn't want to be "It."

Mr. Dennehy and nine of his friends have spent the past 23 years locked in a game of "Tag." It started in high school when they spent their morning break darting around the campus of Gonzaga Preparatory School [Spokane, Washington]. Then they moved on—to college, careers, families and new cities. But because of a reunion, a contract and someone's unusual idea to stay in touch, tag keeps pulling them closer. Much closer.

The game they play is fundamentally the same as the school-yard version: One player is "It" until he tags someone else. But men in their 40s can't easily chase each other around the playground, at least not without making people nervous, so this tag has a twist. There are no geographic restrictions and the game is live for the entire month of February. The last guy tagged stays "It" for the year.

That means players get tagged at work and in bed. They form alliances and fly around the country. Wives are enlisted as spies and assistants are ordered to bar players from the office. "You're like a deer or elk in hunting season," says Joe Tombari, a high-school teacher in Spokane, who sometimes locks the door of his classroom during off-periods and checks under his car before he gets near it. Mr. Tombari was "It" in 1982, heading into the last day of high school. He plotted to tag a friend, who had gone home early that day. But when he got there, the friend, tipped off by another player, was sitting in his parents' car with the doors locked. There wasn't enough time to tag someone else. "The whole thing was quite devastating," says Mr. Tombari. "I was 'It' for life."

But about eight years later, some of the group was gathered for a weekend when the topic turned to Mr. Tombari and the feeble finish to his tag career. Someone came up with an idea to revive the game for one month out of each year. Patrick Schultheis, then a first-year lawyer, drafted a "Tag

Participation Agreement," which outlined the spirit of the game and the rules (no tagging the player who just tagged you). Everyone signed. The game was on.

Over the years, some of the players fanned out around the country—which curbed the action but raised the stakes. At one point, Chris Ammann was living in Boston. So Brian Konesky dipped into his frequent-flier miles and crossed the country on the last weekend of the month. He spent the next two days in the bushes outside Mr. Ammann's apartment, sitting in his friend's favorite bar or driving up and down his street. Mr. Ammann never showed. Mr. Konesky was "It" for the year.

"I felt bad," says Mr. Ammann, who had gone out of town for the weekend. "I think I would have sacrificed getting tagged just to spend some time with him."[62]

Over the past couple of years, I have read that story to a number of different audiences—men's groups, youth gatherings, and broadly mixed audiences. When I look out at the crowd, they are all smiling. The grins are real, wide and genuine. People's eyes are lit up with excitement.

Why does that story engage us so much? The answer is in the last sentence. "I think I would have sacrificed getting tagged just to spend some time with him." Why are friendships so important? It is because real friends teach us and develop us. They bless and empower us. That's why we are willing to be "It."

GOD EXPECTS AND EMPOWERS US TO STICK WITH OUR FRIENDS (PROVERBS 17:17).

God expects and empowers us to stick with our friends. Look at this wisdom from Proverbs 17:17; 18:24; and 27:10:

A friend is always loyal, and a brother is born to help in time of need.

There are "friends" who destroy each other, but a real friend sticks closer than a brother.

Never abandon a friend—either yours or your father's. Then in your time of need, you won't have to ask your relatives for assistance. (NLT)

God expects us to be loyal friends. That's what people need, and that's the kind of person God uses. Eric Felten wrote a book that I found very interesting. It's titled *Loyalty: The Vexing Virtue*. In the book, Mr. Felten deftly describes the kind of character needed for real friendships to flourish: "It is trust that binds us to the ones we love; without those bonds of loyalty the everyday furies of life fling us apart."[63]

He's right. Sadly, faithless behavior is much more common than loyalty, isn't it? Such has always been the case, but our time has a new wrinkle. One of the common occurrences of our day is watching person A blab online about person B. A is unhappy because B doesn't seem faithful to A's concept of fairness, therefore A excoriates B in public. People do this about companies, governments, spouses, and their children. We are so quick to pounce on another's disloyalty that we are blind to our *own* faithlessness.

King David, an expert on loyal love, captured the situation perfectly in Psalm 55:20-21:

He has put forth his hands against those who were at peace
with him;
He has violated his covenant. His speech was smoother
than butter,
But his heart was war; his words were softer than oil,
yet they were drawn swords. (NASB)

Who has caused David such pain here? Is it an enemy? No. If it were, David says it wouldn't cut so deeply. No, this is a friend—and not Jonathan. God expects and empowers us to be loyal friends, to be with others like He is with us; but humans are often too full of insecure self to stay that course. Instead, we rend each other with words that are weapons.

This happens even inside God's covenant community. We read verses 13-14 of that same psalm:

But it is you, a man my equal,
My companion and my familiar friend.
We who had sweet fellowship together,
walked in the house of God in the throng. (NASB)

Such disloyalty tears up not only the one we blast. It eats at our own insides as well. The disloyal one and the one he wounds are each left weeping.

THERE IS HEALING FOR THOSE WOUNDED BY FAITHLESS FRIENDS (PSALM 55:22-23).

Thankfully, there is judgment for transgressors and healing for those wounded by faithless friends. Look at the end of David's song, in verses 22 and 23:

Cast your burden upon the LORD, and He will sustain you;
He will never allow the righteous to be shaken.
But Thou, O God, wilt bring them down to the pit of destruction;
Men of bloodshed and deceit will not live out half their days.
But I will trust in Thee. (NASB)

My former boss Dan Bolin is now President of Christian Camping International. He is a great leader and friend, and recently shared a fascinating comment on this idea:

A few weeks ago I heard a captivating presentation by a man who had rowed across the Atlantic Ocean with his teenage son. The 82-day adventure, challenge, and bonding were inspirational and exciting. One interesting feature was that their boat was designed to right itself if it happened to turn over. Rough seas, a rogue wave, or even a whale surfacing could flip and swamp the boat. But the design was such that it would not stay overturned for long; the boat would correct its problem and return to its upright position. David knew what it was like to have his life turned upside down. But he also knew that God is in the business of righting overturned lives.[64]

Friends, listen carefully. If your life has been capsized by sin, disappointment, or the trauma of faithless friendship; remember that your soul is like that boat. God wants to right your ship and set you rowing safely once again. Of course, the practical question is "How?" How does God right our boat? How can I learn to make friends again and be the friend God intends when I have been burned and burned others so often?" Those questions take us to our next big idea.

MENTORING IS CRITICALLY IMPORTANT.

Men (and women) aren't just meant to bond with peers. Mentoring is also part of healthy male development, and mentoring plays a big role in righting our boats. There are two aspects of mentoring that really help us grow up into the God's idea of friends. The first kind is called active mentoring, a direct engagement between protégé and mentor who know each other. 2 Timothy 2:1-2 is one of the many texts that calls us to engage in active mentoring.

> You therefore, my son, be strong in the grace that is in Christ Jesus. And the things which you have heard from me in the presence of many witnesses, these entrust to faithful men, who will be able to teach others also. (NASB)

Don't you love the legacy in that command? Look at the multi-generational aspects: Paul actively trains Timothy to be strong, Tim passes that strength on to others he mentors, and they in turn disciple others. It's awesome! And it's why you and I feel such kinship with Christians who preceded us by hundreds of years.

Whether it is a skill, an attitude, a way of seeing, or the practice of following Jesus—our job is to help other people grow up. It's part of being a real friend. It's also an important way to overcome the disappointments of life. We press on and pass on the good. But, I must confess to a little trepidation on this point. Modern men have become lazy and inhabit a culture that glorifies victimization and effeminacy. I wonder and fear whether modern men will be able to pass on the greatness of Christian discipleship. I fear we'll be like the Dad on a car commercial from a few years back. The misguided but well-intentioned father was teaching his son to throw a baseball, but the man himself threw in a painfully weak and effeminate fashion. So many good, Christian guys are training their sons to throw—and live—like girls. Don't misunderstand. Women are wonderful, important equals, but the males you mentor aren't meant to become women.

Men, instead of repeating that cultural nonsense or other equally idiotic models like macho gangs, let's practice active biblical mentoring. Find some older and wiser Christian man who has time to spend with you. Meet on regular occasions together and learn from him how to live out Scripture like a biblical man. And please, don't ask your pastor or anyone to find a mentor for you. If young elephants can find their own mentors, you can do the same. Just keep asking until God provides a wiser fellow who has the time to meet with you. Then, pass that on to others. Go get a Timothy of your own, or two or three. Engage in active mentoring as God commands.

WE SHOULD ENGAGE WITH PASSIVE MENTORING (ROMANS 15:4).

The second type of discipleship is passive. We men should also engage with passive mentoring. That's part of the brilliance in Romans 15:4. Paul writes:

> … whatever was written in earlier times was written for our instruction, that through perseverance and the encouragement of the Scriptures we might have hope. (NASB)

The stories in the Bible aren't just tales of wonder or mere historical records. They are God's words that pierce and change our lives. When we engage with God's Word, it really does make all the difference in our lives. People like Paul and Timothy become mentors to us.

Of course, the same holds true for people outside the Bible. We can learn from all of God's world—actively being developed even by people we could never meet. That's passive mentoring. We learn from those who are far away in time or space and incorporate their lessons into our lives.

A generation ago, Paul Stanley and Bob Clinton came up with a really easy way to remember all this. Looking at the Bible, they said that God expects each person to develop according to a constellation model.[65] Our active and passive mentoring should form a kind of cross, as in the Orion or Southern Cross constellations.

There are people "above" us so to speak. Those who have gone before but who influence us through active mentoring or shape us passively through their writing, videos, or legacy. Then, there are people coming after us, whom we actively mentor or passively shape through our own contributions. These "above" and "below" mentors and disciples comprise the vertical axis. The horizontal axis is made up of our peer friends—both inside and outside our normal organization. These also help us grow into the people God wants us to be and to fully mature.

Altogether, these friendships shape our lives. We should curry these friendships as if we were walking on a mountain with them, tied together for the well-being of all. After all, we need each other and God expects us to grow together inside and outside our normal groups and across the generations. If you'd like to get some specific direction in this area, I highly recommend Dennis Rainey's book *Stepping Up*, mentioned in Chapter 2. Dennis talks about becoming a modern patriarch through friendship and mentoring in a simple, engaging way.

MARRIAGE IS CRITICALLY IMPORTANT.

Of course, we won't have done justice to the subject of friendship if we don't address the most significant friend of all—one's spouse.

A MAN IS BLESSED WHO HAS A COMPLETING LIFE PARTNER (PROVERBS 31:10-12).

For a man whom God intends to be married, there is no friendship more important than his spouse. And a man is blessed who has a completing life partner. Read Proverbs 31:10-12 on this topic:

An excellent wife, who can find?
For her worth is far above jewels.
The heart of her husband trusts in her,
and he will have no lack of gain.

She does him good and not evil
all the days of her life. (NASB)

Don't misread the rhetorical nature of the opening question. *The Living Bible* ignores the actual terms but captures better the intended meaning:

> If you can find a truly good wife, she is worth more than precious gems! Her husband can trust her, and she will richly satisfy his needs. She will not hinder him but help him all her life. (TLB)

Not long ago, I was in Michigan, performing the wedding ceremony for one of our pastors and his bride. As a staff, we had been mercilessly teasing this great young man about his long engagement. The youth staff kept counting off the remaining days on his office board for months. He took it all in stride, as I had expected because this fellow was clearly aware that he was being blessed with something the worth of which is beyond measure. When the day finally came, he was overjoyed to stand on that stage before God and say, "Forsaking all others, I cleave only unto you."

A MAN IS SUPPOSED TO GIVE HIS LIFE FOR HIS WIFE (EPHESIANS 5:28-30).

In those marriage vows, our young pastor was trying to summarize something God's people have been saying for millennia: that a man is giving his life for his wife. It's what Paul teaches so effectively in Ephesians 5 when he writes in verses 28-30:

> In the same way [that Jesus loves the church] husbands are to love their wives as their own bodies. He who loves his wife loves himself. For no one ever hates his own flesh but provides and cares for it, just as Christ does for the church, since we are members of His body. (HCSB)

"As Christ loves the church." Think on that for a moment, would you? I see four really big aspects to this:

#1—This is permanent. After all, is Jesus' love a temporary thing? Is it here today and gone tomorrow? What does Jesus say about those He bonds to Him? In John 10 we hear Jesus saying, "I have them in my hand and no one shall take them from Me." Gentlemen, if your love is fickle, if it wanes with the actions or attitudes of your wife, then you are not loving as Jesus loves. His love is permanent.

Now, you may be thinking, "You don't know my wife!" You're right. I don't. But I know Jesus. And I know that He empowers you to love like He does, regardless of what comes your way.. And if He can love you, then He can surely enable you to love your wife. Eric Felten chimes in on this in his *Loyalty* book:

> Love that isn't inspired by the possibility of permanence is no sort of love at all. No one dreams of someday "hooking up." We aren't riveted by tales of lovers who are indifferent to the question of whether their relationship will last ... To say that someone is "afraid of commitment" is to say that he isn't in any significant way [loving] at all.[66]

#2—That takes us to the second things that jumps out from Ephesians 5: love must be the dominant trait in one's character. Think about it. 1 John 4 reminds us that "God is love." Jesus loves us permanently because it's the dominant trait in His divine character. As ones being made into His image, we are also supposed to be so full of love that it can't help but flow out of us. We are to love like Jesus, who is—in a word—love.

In fact, it's the reason I teach. It's why you and I study together. As Paul summarized in 1 Timothy 1:5, love is the whole goal of our instruction. Without love, we are nothing (see 1 Corinthians 13).

#3—This requires dying to self, which is point number three. Friend, Jesus died on a cross, willingly laying down His life so that your sins could no longer separate you from the Holy God. Jesus died a grisly death for you. That is what real men and real women do. They lay down their lives for the ones they love.

One of the things that gives me great joy is hearing the manifold ways men live this out today. I meet lots of men serving in their church's ministries. I see men laying their lives down for their wives. I hear from men giving money to God's work. I read about guys encouraging and promoting others. Frankly, it is all stirring and beautiful.

#4—That bring us to point four from Ephesians 5: following Jesus requires serving and leading. Jesus rose from the dead so that all who trust in Him might follow Him, partnering with Him in a life walk. In the same way, God expects us men to serve and lead our homes such that our wives partner with us in a life walk after Jesus. And that is ultimately what it means to give your life for your wife—you know her and help her become all God intends her to be. You don't merely die for her. You live for her.

Author Susan Foh has a powerful word on this:

> The husband's chief duty is to love his wife as Christ loved the church. The most common description of Christ's love in this context is "self-sacrificing." Christ's love for the church is self-sacrificing with a purpose—to sanctify and present her to Himself in splendor, without blemish. And so the husband is to nourish and cherish his wife. He is to do for his wife what he would do for himself. He is to encourage her growth in the image of Christ and to help her develop and use her gifts. But how does one do that? Like Jesus. Christ knows His bride's needs and how to meet them; He knows what her goal is and how to reach it.[67]

How does one act like Jesus? You do so by knowing the goals and needs and desires of your bride, something that requires study and questioning and honest communication without gamesmanship.

A MAN IS SUPPOSED TO TREASURE HIS WIFE (1 PETER 3:7).

With this, we come to our final point: A man is supposed to treasure his wife. Such is what we read in 1 Peter 3:7:

> You husbands likewise, live with your wives in an understanding way, as with a weaker vessel, since she is a woman; and grant her honor as a fellow heir of the grace of life, so that your prayers may not be hindered. (NASB)

Three really significant Greek words occur here. *Sungkleronomos* is what we render "fellow heir." It's a cool word that's hard to get into other languages. It combines *sun*—a deep word for togetherness—with *kleronomos*. *Kleronomos* is itself a combo term, and it means "to possess." Therefore, the word God chose means "to possess together."

Specifically, a husband and wife are in marriage together as a team. They are deeply bound together in the deepest of all friendships. They are joint possessors of God's grace. Think about the implications of that! How far does one get in a three-legged race if he cripples the partner? Not very far. Gentlemen, look at what the Bible is saying. You better *treasure* your wife! Otherwise, you are trying to run the race with dead weight, and not a partner. You will be hindered in every way. Even your prayers will fall flat.

Our second awesome word is *sunoikeo*, what we translate "live." Does the first part sound familiar? It's *sun* again, the deep connection word. *Oikos* is a house and *oikeo* means to live in a house. Married men and women, this is saying that you are commanded to live one life together. You are to really live as best buddies, deeply connected as one house. As Moses condensed it: the two shall become one. That leaves no room for separate agendas, private friends, and closed bank accounts. You are to live one life as one house.

This takes a great deal of work, but the rewards are almost unfathomably rich. Like you, my sweetheart and I have busy and full lives. Some days we come home late and are exhausted. Yet we do not go to sleep until we have talked at a real level of sharing. We don't merely share all the events of the day, but how we felt about them and what we feared, enjoyed, failed at, etc. This means that some nights we are talking until 2:00 am. I still must arise early for my morning swim and get to work, but it's worth it to really live *sunoikeo*.

Our final revealing Greek phrase is *kata gnoosin*—what we portray in English as "in an understanding way." That's a great translation, provided we are sure to grasp the kind of understanding meant. It's not "understanding" in the English sense of being kind or forgiving; though that's wonderful. *Gnosis* means knowledge, specifically observable knowledge. It's what we would call scientific understanding. In other words, a guy needs to study his wife all the time. He must become an expert in the science of his closest friend.

Don Meredith leads the Joe Gibbs Racing team and has a great comment on this:

> Peter is commanding us to be experts about our wives. Most successful husbands I know make it a point to ask their wives about their emotional, physical and spiritual needs ... Do you know what a perfect day is for your wife? A perfect date? What she *really* likes to do on vacations? If not, you'd better find out! Peter commands us to know our wives and to allow them access to us.[68]

Men need to cultivate real relationships. Of course our natural sin tendencies and culturally-reinforced negative stereotypes with make the process difficult. It is not easy to foster friendships. They require great effort and commitment. Yet such is a small price to pay for honoring God. You see, when we give ourselves to friendships, we mirror the beautiful Triunity of God. He exists as Three Persons in relationship and develops us to enjoy a similar blessing—relating rightly with our peers, mentors, protégés, spouses, and Him.

ACTION STEPS

Thank you for the privilege of working together on this journey. Though my engagement with you through this book has reached an end, there are many action steps that can help you continue to grow in godly manhood.

Where do you go from here? What's next if you are serious about the material in this book? Here are some essentials:

Find a mentor. As we discussed in the last chapter, I highly recommend you do the hard work of finding a mentor. Your church is a perfect place for this, as it places you in community even after the mentoring season is complete. You should also find a "Timothy" whom you can disciple as well.

Pursue personal study. Should you want to continue learning and thinking about manhood, look at the Recommended Reading at the end of this book and choose one to start reading.

Join a group study. A regular Bible study group can be a rich and important tool in spiritual growth. If your church has men's study groups, you may want to recommend this study, using the DVDs and workbooks available through All The Difference. www.allthedifference.us or Lampion Press. If your church doesn't have a regular men's Bible study, possibly this could serve as a good launch for you.

Engage routinely in reflection, application, and worship. Please make certain that you are completing the Bible study process. The point of all Bible study is to grow in love (1 Timothy 1:5). Therefore, we must take each lesson learned and pray it through, discussing it with the Triune God whose Spirit reveals the way our lives can change as a result. As we apply these changes, it can lead to beautiful responses of worship, praising our God who is love. For example, my son responded to this series by writing the following poetry:

To Be a Man of God

My father reminds me that my body is not my own
I am just a vessel to spread his glory
I will not leave a single surface untouched
I shall not leave a single soul unblessed
It is our great commission

Did you ever think that you would be this blessed
To have a path laid out before you
Freedom is yours and it's up to you to choose
To be a man of God
Or get lost in your own shoes

Each gift is yours with what to do
I choose to use mine for his word
To spread and not get lost in my own shoes
I know now what I must do
I hope that all of you will follow as he guides us to a brighter tomorrow

Michael Braudrick[69]

Know that we are all for you. Before you ever picked up this book, people prayed for you. All of us who worked on this project have been humbled and encouraged by the blessing of godly manhood, and we pray that you experience the same. Personally, I want to thank you for the honor of studying the Bible with you and thinking together through such a momentous topic. My hope is that you and I and those we engage will better the world through the power of biblical manhood.

Remember the big ideas. So, what have we read in this study? What's the bottom line? Very simply, it is this:

A real man keeps his word.
A real man keeps his focus.
A real man serves and leads.
A real man fights for right.
A real man thinks and learns.
A real man makes real friends.

That's it. It is simple, but it is not easy. Yet, with God's help it can be done!

ENDNOTES

1   Cited in Hanna Rosin, *The End of Men and the Rise of Women* (New York: Riverhead Book, 2012), 13.

2   G. C. Dilsaver *The Three Marks of Manhood: How to be Priest, Prophet and King of Your Family* (Charlotte, NC: TAN Books, 2014), 56.

3   Ibid., 58.

4   Ibid., 59

5   Personal correspondence to author of 26 July 2014.

6   Charles Murray, "Why Economics Can't Explain Our Cultural Divide" *Wall Street Journal*, 16 March 2012 (Life & Style) cited in personal correspondence to author, 18 January 2014.

7   Survey results and figures come from 29 October 2009 report chaired by Rich Jarc of the Josephson Institute and reviwed by Rick Hesse of Pepperdine University.

8   Foundation For Life. *Mid-High Teacher's Resource 2006* (Washington, D.C.: Character Counts!, 2006), 3. Research performed by the Josephson Institute in association with The Templeton Foundation and republished 4 January 2013 on the Josephson Institute website.

9   John Cowan, *Small Decencies* (New York: HarperCollins, 1993), 41.

10 Mary Eberstadt, "Adam and Eve After The Pill," *Wall Street Journal*, 1 November 2012, (Life and Style).

11 Crawford Loritts, "Introduction" in Dennis Rainey, *Stepping Up: A Call to Courageous Manhood* (Little Rock: FamilyLife Publishing, 2011), 7.

12 Jackie Kendall, *A Man Worth Waiting For: How to Avoid a Bozo* (New York: FaithWords, 2008), 184.

13 "CIA Chief Resigns," *Wall Street Journal,* 10 November 2012, Front page Note: As of this writing, General Petraeus was also having difficulty for other failings in faithfulness. He was fined $100,000 and given probation for sharing access to military secrets with his mistress. (See *The Washington Post,* "Sentencing," 24 April 2015, A-1.).

14 Doug Cameron *"Kubasik Out on Ethics,"* Wall Street Journal, 10 November 2012, Business.

15 Cowan, *Small Decencies,* 148-49.

16 This is a common trope among collegiate feminists, most famously espoused by the character Val in Marilyn French's novel *The Women's Room.* She says, "Whatever they may be in public life, whatever their relations with men, in their relations with women, all men are rapists, and that's all they are. They rape us with their eyes, their laws, and their codes." Marilyn French, *The Women's Room* (New York: Ballantine, 1988), 19.

17 Adam Carolla, *In Fifty Years We'll All Be Chicks* (New York: Crown, 2010), 1, 100.

18 Kathleen Connelly and Martin Heesacker, "Why is Benevolent Sexism Appealing?" *Psychology of Women Quarterly* 36:4 (December 2012): 433.

19 Ibid., 440.

20 Charles Murray, *American Enterprise Institute Bulletin,* 29 November 2012, 1.

21 Ken Gire, *Relentless Pursuit* (Bloomington, MN: Bethany House, 2012), 26.

22 Keith Ablow, *"We are raising a generation of deluded narcissists"*, *Fox News* 08 January 2013.

23 See Matthew 14:23 and Galatians 5:22-23.

24 Personal correspondence to author in the author's files.

25 Dennis Rainey, *Stepping Up: A Call to Courageous Manhood* (Little Rock: FamilyLife Publishing, 2011), 170.

26 Howard Hendricks, personal conversation with the author.

27 Stu Weber, *Tender Warrior: Every Man's Purpose, Every Woman's Dream, Every Child's Hope* (Portland: Multnomah Press, 1996) 140-41.

28 Max Lucado, *God Came Near* (Nashville: Thomas Nelson, 1986) 161.

29 Erma Bombeck, *Family—The Ties that Bind ... and Gag* (New York: Random, 1987) 2-3.

30 David Simmonds, personal correspondence with author in author's files and used by permission.

31 Gene Getz, *The Measure of a Man* (Grand Rapids: Baker, 2004), 7.

32 Family Research Council, Patrick F. Fagan, Ph.D. and Althea Nagai, Ph.D. "Mapping America" multiple studies published by marriResearch January 20, 2015. Similar findings come from Samantha Litzinger and Kristina Coop Gordon, "Exploring Relationships Among Communication, Sexual Satisfaction, and Marital Satisfaction," *Journal of Sex and Marital Therapy* 31, no. 5 (2005): 409-24.

33 Robert Lewis, *Raising A Modern-Day Knight: A Father's Role in Guiding His Son to Authentic Manhood.* Revised and Engarged Edition.Carol Stream, IL: Tyndale House Publishers, 2007. For daughters, see Pam Ferrel and Doreen Hanna, *Raising a Modern-Day Princess: Inspiring Purpose, Value, and Strength in Your Daughter.* Carol Stream, IL: Tyndale House Publishers, 2009.

34 Randall Satchell, personal correspondence with author in author's files and used by permission.

35 Michael Craven, Crosswalk.com web post 11 June 2012.

36 Werner Haug and Phillipe Warner, "The Demographic Characteristics of the Linguistic and Religious Groups in Switzerland" *Population Studies 2* (2000), 2.

37 Ibid., 7.

38 Ibid., 9.

39 Ibid., 19.

40 Kay S.Hymnowitz, *Manning Up: How the Rise of Women Has Turned Men into Boys* (New York: Basic Books, 2012), 22.

41 Ibid., 43-44.

42 Stephen J. Bramer, "Kinsman-Redeemer" in *Baker's Evangelical Dictionary of Biblical Theology*. Walter A. Elwell, ed. (Grand Rapids: Baker Books, 1996), 167.

43 Ibid., 167-68.

44 James Dobson, *Bringing Up Boys* (Carol Stream, IL: Tyndale, 2001), 246.

45 Rodney Stark, *How the West Won: The Neglected Story of the Triumph of Modernity* (Wilmington, Delaware: ISI, 2014), 68.

46 *Lars and the Real Girl,* written by Nancy Oliver and directed by Craig Gillespie (Metro Goldwyn Mayer, 2007).

47 David Grossman, *On Killing: The Psychological Cost of Learning to Kill in War and Society* (New York: Little, Brown, and Company, 1995) 184-85.

48 Personal correspondence to the author of 15 January 2013.

49 Personal correspondence to the author 23 February 2013.

50   Steve Lawson, *Men Who Win:Pursuing the Ultimate Prize* (Colorado Springs: Navpress, 1992) 28-29.

51   C. S. Lewis, *The Abolition of Man* (New York: HarperCollins 1974) 26.

52   *The Economist*, January 12th-18th 2013.

53   Personal correspondence to the author used with permission.

54   Henry David Thoreau, *Walden* (Stillwell, KS: Digireads 2005) 67.

55   Theodore Gray "For That Healthy Glow, Drink Radiation!" *Popular Science*, August 2004, 28.

56   Personal correspondence to the author in author's files.

57   Richard Wurmbrand, *Tortured for Christ* (Middlebury, IN: Living Sacrifice Books, 1976), 184.

58   Caitlin O'Connell-Rodwell, "How Male Elephants Bond," *Smithsonian* (November 2010), 52.

59   Homer, *The Illiad*, Book X.

60   David Wade, personal letter to the author in the author's files, used with permission.

61   A. D. Nuttall, *Shakespeare the Thinker* (New Haven, Connecticut: Yale University Press, 2011), 106.

62   Russell Adams "It Takes Planning, Caution to Avoid Being 'It,'" *Wall Street Journal* 28 January 2013, 1.

63   Eric Felten, *Loyalty: The Vexing Virtue* (New York: Simon and Schuster, 2011), 129.

64   Dan Bolin, "Fresh Bread," Newsletter 21 March 2011.

65   See J. Robert Clinton and Paul D. Stanley, *Connecting: The Mentoring Relationships You Need to Succeed in Life.* Colorado Springs: NavPress, 1992.

[66] Eric Felten, *Loyalty: The Vexing Virtue* (New York: Simon and Schuster, 2011), 144.

[67] Susan T. Foh, *Women and the Word of God* (Grand Rapids: Baker Books, 1980), 201-202.

[68] Don Meredith, *Becoming One* (Nashville: Thomas Nelson, 1979), 134.

[69] Used with permission.

RECOMMENDED READING

Bailey, Kenneth. *Jesus Through Middle Eastern Eyes.* Downer's Grove, Illinois: InterVarsity Press, 2008.

Beltz, Bob. *Daily Disciplines for the Christian Man.* Colorado Springs: Navpress, 1993.

Dobson, James. *Bringing Up Boys.* Carol Stream, Illinois: Tyndale, 2005.

_____. *Straight Talk to Men and Their Wives.* Waco: Word, 1980.

Farrar, Steve. *Point Man.* Portland, OR: Multnomah, 2003.

Getz, Gene. *The Measure of a Man.* Grand Rapids: Baker, 2004.

Heald, Jack and Cynthia Heald. *Loving Your Wife.* Colorado Springs: NavPress, 1989.

Hendricks, Howard and William Hendricks. *As Iron Sharpens Iron: Building Character in a Mentoring Relationship.* Chicago: Moody Press, 1995.

Hicks, Robert. *The Masculine Journey.* Colorado Springs: Navpress, 1993.

Hymowitz, Kay S. *Manning Up: How the Rise of Women Has Turned Men Into Boys.* New York: Basic Books, 2012.

Kimmel, Michael. *Guyland: The Perilous World where Boys Become Men.* New York: HarperCollins, 2008.

Lawson, Steve. *Men Who Win:Pursuing the Ultimate Prize.* Colorado Springs: NavPress 1992.

Lewis, Robert and William Hendricks, *Rocking the Roles.* Colorado Springs: NavPress, 2003.

McCartney, Bill, ed., *What Makes a Man?* Colorado Springs: NavPress, 1992.

McDowell, Kevin. *Samson of a Man.* Enumclaw, WA: Winepress, 2007.

Morley, Patrick. *The Seven Seasons of the Man in the Mirror.* Grand Rapids: Zondervan, 2010.

Nuttall, A. D. *Shakespeare the Thinker.* New Haven, CT: Yale University Press, 2011.

Parsons, Rob. *The Sixty Minute Family.* Oxford, UK: Lion Hudson, 2010.

Rainey, Dennis. *Stepping Up: A Call to Courageous Manhood.* Little Rock, AR: Family Life Publishing, 2011.

Rosin, Hannah. *The End of Men And the Rise of Women.* New York: Riverhead Book, 2012.

Schmidt, Alvin J. *How Christianity Changed the World.* Grand Rapids: Zondervan, 2004.

Stanley Paul D. and Robert J. Clinton, *Connecting: The Mentoring Relationships You Need to Succeed in Life.* Colorado Springs: NavPress, 1992.

Weber, Stu *Tender Warrior: Every Man's Purpose, Every Woman's Dream, Every Child's Hope.* Portland, OR: Multnomah Press, 1996.

ABOUT THE AUTHOR

Wayne Braudrick serves as Senior Pastor of Frisco Bible Church in Frisco, Texas. He also teaches on many radio stations through the *All the Difference* daily broadcast and serves as adjunct faculty for Ouachita Baptist University. Dr. Braudrick earned his doctorate in leadership communication through Middlesex University in London. He gained a master's degree in biblical studies at Dallas Theological Seminary; and was a National Merit Scholar at Baylor University where he read history, literature, and education. Wayne lives with his marvelous family in Frisco, Texas, where he and his wife refuse to let work come in the way of their regular racquetball games.

ALSO AVAILABLE:

DIG DEEPER WITH THE COMPANION
STUDY GUIDE!

ALSO AVAILABLE FROM LAMPION PRESS

LOOK FOR THESE AND OTHER
GREAT TITLES AT: LAMPIONPRESS.COM